Ahmedabad

A Study in Indian Urban History

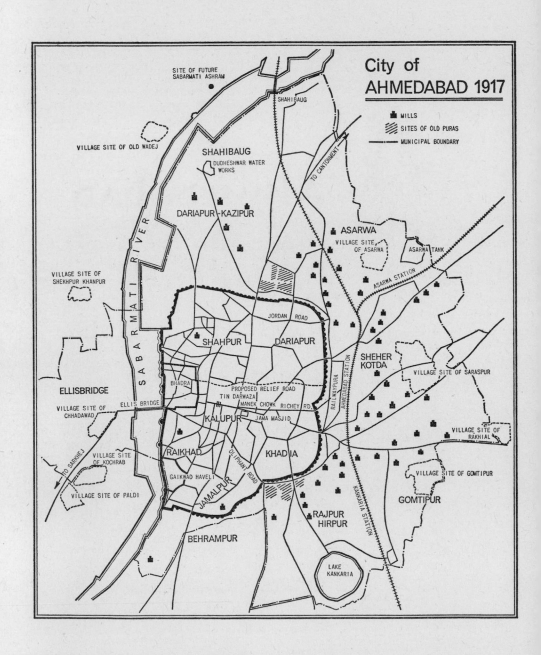

City of
AHMEDABAD 1917

MILLS
SITES OF OLD PURAS
MUNICIPAL BOUNDARY

SITE OF FUTURE
SABARMATI ASHRAM

SHAHIBAUG

VILLAGE SITE OF OLD WADEJ

SHAHIBAUG

DUDHESHWAR WATER
WORKS

DARIAPUR-KAZIPUR

TO CANTONMENT

ASARWA

VILLAGE SITE
OF ASARWA

ASARWA TANK

VILLAGE SITE OF
SHEKHPUR KHANPUR

SABARMATI RIVER

ASARWA STATION

JORDAN ROAD

SHAHPUR

DARIAPUR

SHEHER
KOTDA

VILLAGE SITE OF SARASPUR

BHADRA

PROPOSED RELIEF ROAD

RAILWAYPURA

AHMEDABAD STATION

ELLISBRIDGE

ELLIS BRIDGE

TIN DARWAZA

MANEK CHOWK RICHEY RD.

VILLAGE SITE OF
CHHADAWAD

KALUPUR

JAMA MASJID

VILLAGE SITE OF
RAKHIAL

TO SARKHEJ

VILLAGE SITE
OF KOCHRAB

RAIKHAD

KHADIA

OLIPHANT ROAD

GAIKWAD HAVELI

VILLAGE SITE OF GOMTIPUR

VILLAGE SITE OF PALDI

JAMALPUR

KANKARIA STATION

GOMTIPUR

BEHRAMPUR

RAJPUR
HIRPUR

LAKE
KANKARIA

Ahmedabad

A Study in Indian Urban History

Kenneth L. Gillion

University of California Press

Berkeley and Los Angeles · 1968

UNIVERSITY OF CALIFORNIA PRESS
BERKELEY AND LOS ANGELES, CALIFORNIA

CAMBRIDGE UNIVERSITY PRESS
LONDON, ENGLAND

LIBRARY OF CONGRESS CATALOG CARD NUMBER: 68–25943
PRINTED IN THE UNITED STATES OF AMERICA

To my Mother and Father

Acknowledgments

My obligations to others in the preparation of this study are considerable: to the University of Adelaide for leave to make three visits to India and to Ahmedabad and the study leave during which the manuscript was written; to the Australian National University and the Ford Foundation for financial assistance towards the visits to India and particularly to Dr. D. A. Low, who arranged it; to the Maharashtra State Record Office, Ahmedabad Municipal Corporation, National Archives of India, and India Office Library for granting me access to their records; to the Librarians of the Bombay University, the Asiatic Society of Bombay, the Cama Oriental Institute in Bombay, the National Library in Calcutta, the Ahmedabad Textile Industry's Research Association, Gujarat

Vidyapith, Gujarat Vidya Sabha, Maneklal Jethabhai, and Millowners' Association Libraries in Ahmedabad, and the Federation of Indian Chambers of Commerce and Industry and the Indian School of International Studies Libraries in New Delhi; to Arvind Desai, S. R. Bharucha, and S. Zaveri, for translations from Gujarati; to Yashodhar Mehta for putting several rare books at my disposal; to Dinker Trivedi, Proprietor of the New Order Book Company, who provided indispensable help in introducing me to Ahmedabad; to Milton Singer and Bernard Cohn of the University of Chicago for help in various ways during and after a study-tour of American centres of Indian Studies sponsored by the Carnegie Corporation; to Mrs. Edna Hawke for typing the manuscript; and to others whose kindness and helpfulness made this work a pleasure.

NOTES

Complete author's names, titles, and publication data are given in the Bibliography, pp. 178–189; a roman numeral I, II, or III indicates the section of the Bibliography in which the work is listed. The following abbreviations are used in the Notes; all but the last one, *P.P.*, refer to unpublished official documents of the Bombay Government.

F. D.   Financial Department
G. D.   General Department
J. D.   Judicial Department
P. D.   Political Department
R. D.   Revenue Department
S. D.   Secret Department
P. P.   *Parliamentary Papers*

Contents

Introduction

Modern Indian historiography no longer confines its study to the activities of rulers. The Indian nationalist movement is receiving close attention from scholars in several countries, as are the effects of British law and land revenue settlements on the social structure of rural India. But those who wish to read about Indian cities are still more likely to look to the works of geographers and sociologists than to those of historians. This book is a preliminary excursion into Indian urban history. It is not intended to be a contribution to urban theory. It draws to some extent on work in the other social sciences, some general discussion and comparisons are included, and the pertinence of general theoretical concepts is kept in mind (if not always explicitly discussed). However, it is not

primarily a book about Indian cities in general, but one about
the unique experience of a particular city.

Ahmedabad, the capital of Gujarat, was chosen for study
because it is both an old city—once the most splendid in India—
and a modern industrial city—now India's sixth largest, with
a population of more than one and a quarter millions, and per
capita one of the richest. Unlike Bombay, Calcutta, Madras,
and Kanpur, Ahmedabad was not a creation of the British, but
a city which, while remaining true to itself, successfully adapted
to the new industrial age, carrying over commercial and industrial skills and patterns of traditional social organization.
In no great city of India can the continuity of past and present
be seen as clearly as in Ahmedabad, and it is continuity, rather
than change, which is emphasized in this book.

Ahmedabad is neither a well-known nor a much loved
city. Since the seventeenth century it has been as much neglected by visitors as by writers. Its utilitarian and parochial
spirit does not attract outsiders, while the Ahmedabadis are
too modest and too busy to try to put the rest of the world
right about their interesting city. The situation today is as it
was in 1868 when the English social reformer, Mary Carpenter,
wrote in praise of Ahmedabad: "This extraordinary city is so
little known on the other side of India, that when at Calcutta
some months afterwards, I spoke to an educational inspector
about schools in Ahmedabad, he remarked, 'You may as well
speak in England of what is done in the school of some remote
village in Russia, as to us here of such a place as Ahmedabad.' "[1]
The eulogies of Ahmedabad's architecture which appear in the
standard guides do not attract tourists. Murray's Guide states:
"It is hard to account for the scant attention paid to Ahmedabad by modern travellers from Europe unless its reputation
as an industrial centre and the fact that there has been prohibi-

[1] M. Carpenter, I, 37 (III).

tion there since 1938 has deterred them.''[2] But the neglect is not new. Tourists fly over Ahmedabad, "scrambling on to Agra and Delhi" as they did in 1890 when Caine wrote in his guide to India, "Ahmedabad is one of the most beautiful and picturesque cities in India and no traveller should pass it by."[3] Scholars, too, have avoided this city, which has been an exception to many of the statements commonly made about India and Indian history.

This book reflects my conviction that in the study of Indian history not enough attention has been paid until recently to regional differences within India. Most of the generalizations made about Indian history are more applicable to Bengal or Hindustan than to Gujarat. The British came to Bengal earlier; many of the great issues of British policy in India were fought out there; several famous historians have written about Bengal; and a very high proportion of India's own historians are Bengalis. Indian historical studies have, in short, been dominated by Bengali themes and historians of Bengal. But Gujarat is not Bengal; if its experience in modern times has been different, this has been due not only to different external pressures, but also to differences in her traditional cultural pattern.

Situated between the Arabian Sea and the kingdoms of central and northern India, possessed of a long coastline and fertile soil, Gujarat for more than two thousand years has been a centre of trade and textile exports. Its traders and financiers, not its royal officials, nor its landholders and chieftains, nor even its Brahmins, set the tone of society in Gujarat long before modern times and made business valued and more than normally respectable for all. The Gujaratis are perhaps the least other-worldly of all the Indian peoples. In light-hearted

[2] Lothian, p. 160 (III).
[3] Caine, p. 49 (III).

vein, Yashodhar Mehta, writer and playwright of Ahmedabad, has written of his people:

> A poet has sometimes observed that wherever there is a Gujarati there is Gujarat. This may mean anything or nothing, but I may as well say that wherever there is money or even possibility of money, there always is a Gujarati. The lure of money takes him to all parts of the world and to all sorts of things. Wherever he scents money, all his faculties become immensely concentrated and like a yogi he applies all his wonderful powers of concentration to the extent of *samadhi*. God then reveals himself through money and the Gujarati is in ecstasy. He becomes a sort of Paramahamsa, all smiles, sweetness, good words, amiability, etc. He goes on buying and selling, investing and reinvesting, and creates, by his own concentration and perseverance, heaven on earth, if not for all, at least for his family; if not for his family at least for himself. This is not a mean achievement.[4]

The Ahmedabadi is the Gujarati of the Gujaratis.

The traditional cities of India are most often viewed through the eyes of Bernier and other European travellers who visited the Mughal Empire, and in the light of Weberian and Marxist analysis. They are contrasted with the self-governing towns of medieval Europe with their charters, esprit-de-corps, united bourgeoisie, and independent military power. They appear to be disunited, often ephemeral conglomerations of subjects, dependent on the court and the military-official elite, and prevented from free association by caste rivalries and other religious restraints. But Ahmedabad was, to some extent, an exception. Here was a city with a corporate tradition and spirit, an hereditary bourgeois elite, and a history of indigenous financial, commercial, and industrial activity; these facts, which are

[4] Yashodhar Mehta, "About Ourselves with Apologies. We Gujaratis" (III).

very relevant to its modern history, will be examined in Chapter I. Ahmedabad's wealth came from trade and industry, not from parasitic exploitation of the countryside; its handicrafts were independent of the patronage of a single court; its merchants and financiers were wealthy and constituted a superior social stratum in the city, a largely hereditary plutocracy; and, if it did not enjoy urban autonomy on the European model, still the financial power and social position of its wealthy Vanias and the survival there, but not in most other parts of India, of certain old institutions of Indian society—the Nagarseth, or city head, and the *mahajans*, or guilds—ensured that the government of the city was responsive to their wishes. Any explanation of this survival of the ancient urban mercantile values and institutions in Gujarat and Rajasthan must be very speculative. A few possible reasons were: the extensive trade which passed through these regions on the way to northern India, the interest of the rulers in taxing this trade, and hence their favouring of traders and financiers, and, by contrast with the Gangetic Plain, the restriction of the revenue available from agriculture, in Rajasthan by the infertility of the soil, and in Gujarat by the marked political fragmentation and independence of local chieftains.

Ahmedabad was distinctive in another way also. A British officer noted in 1830: "It is a common reproach against our Government in this country, that towns always fall off under us, but Ahmedabad is a most gratifying exception."[5] More recently R. Palme Dutt has written: "The old populous manufacturing towns, Dacca, Murshidabad (which Clive had described in 1757 to be as extensive, populous, and rich as the city of London), Surat and the like were in a few years rendered desolate under the 'pax Britannica' with a completeness which no ravages of the most destructive war or foreign con-

[5] Commissioner's Circuit Report, R.D. 12/293/1830 (I).

quest could have accomplished."[6] In Chapter II we shall first look at the reasons why Ahmedabad was able to survive the British industrial invasion and even recover some of the prosperity it had been losing under Maratha rule, when these other cities were declining, and then consider her response to British rule and the breakdown of her isolation in the second half of the nineteenth century. This chapter will emphasize the limited British influence on Ahmedabad society in the nineteenth century.

Ahmedabad's history provides few illustrations of the familiar themes in general works on Indian history. The revolt of 1857 was a minor event in the history of Ahmedabad, and communalism a minor problem. This city did not succumb to England's laissez-faire. It had no great intellectual renaissance, no dramatic swing towards the West then away from it, but rather a slow and selective adaptation. Neither the Western-educated middle class nor the comprador class fills the centre of the stage here. Rather, Ahmedabad's story is of the survival and transformation of an important traditional centre of trade and industry into a modern industrial city, under the leadership of an indigenous financial and mercantile elite. Chapter III will deal with the steam powered textile industry, which has been responsible for Ahmedabad's modern growth and recovery of greatness and has earned it the title, "The Manchester of India". The distinctive character of Ahmedabad's industrialization and the carry-over of traditional patterns will be stressed. Modern Ahmedabad was built up by Ahmedabadis, not by Englishmen, Marwaris, or Parsis.

In Chapter IV, the changing urban environment and problems of Ahmedabad will be considered, and with it the history of municipal government and improvement in the city. In contrast to its rapid and successful adaptation to the new com-

---

[6] R. Palme Dutt, p. 102 (III).

mercial and industrial order, Ahmedabad's social and political response to the West was delayed and not at first remarkable. Ahmedabad had one of the earliest municipal organizations in India, but this chapter does not tell a story which would differ significantly from that of other second-rank cities in nineteenth century India, except possibly in the civic-mindedness displayed by the old leading families (if not by the voters and elected commissioners, who opposed improvements and brought about the supersession of the Municipality for incompetence). Apart from any intrinsic interest there is in an account of urban problems and administration in an old Indian city in the mofussil, the point of the story is the limited correlation between economic progress and Western influence and social change in nineteenth century Ahmedabad. Until the First World War, Ahmedabad's economic progress was achieved within a society which remained socially conservative and politically backward.

The advent of Mahatma Gandhi, who chose to make his home in Ahmedabad for many years, was to open an important new phase in its history, one of participation in a wider world, but on its own terms. Chapter V will deal with developments in the city since 1916, especially the influence of Mahatma Gandhi on labour relations, the disturbances of 1919, and the role of Sardar Vallabhbhai Patel in municipal affairs. This is necessarily brief. The serious historian is restricted by his sources, and in accordance with the fifty year rule, Bombay Government records were not open after 1916. The period covered in greatest detail in this book is the century between the British annexation in 1817 and 1916.

Several good books on Ahmedabad exist. During the period of 1748 to 1762, Ali Muhammad Khan wrote the *Mirat-i-Ahmadi*, a detailed account of the history and decline of the city. In 1851 Maganlal Vakhatchand was awarded a prize by the Gujarat Vernacular Society for his *Amdavadno Itihasa*

(*History of Ahmedabad*). In 1879 an excellent gazetteer on
Ahmedabad city and district was published by the Bombay
Government. It was written by government officers, especially
Mr. F. S. P. Lely, and was based on local information, printed
books, and on government records, some of which no longer
exist. In general, the gazetteers of the Bombay Presidency are
better than those of Bengal, being more detailed, based on
wider research, and provided with footnote references. The
Ahmedabad gazetteer was used extensively by Ratnamanirao
Bhimrao Jhote for his monumental *Gujaratnu Patnagar—
Amdavad* (*Ahmedabad, the Capital of Gujarat*), a scholarly
work published in 1929 which made use of most of the published accounts of Ahmedabad and personal observation as
well, capturing the spirit of the city in a way that it is difficult
for an outsider to do. Ratnamanirao's book is now being edited
for republication by the Gujarat Vidya Sabha. In 1937 Mr.
B. K. Boman-Behram published *The Rise of Municipal Government in the City of Ahmedabad*, a comprehensive and accurate collection of documents from the Bombay (now the
Maharashtra State) Record Office, pertaining to local self-
government in Ahmedabad up to 1875. There can be few
cities in the world which have such a published compilation.
Finally, the premier historian of Gujarat, Professor M. S.
Commissariat, has in two volumes of *A History of Gujarat*
(1938, 1957) described Ahmedabad as it was in the days of
Muslim rule. The third and last volume, yet to appear, will deal
with the Maratha period. My work builds on the books named,
asks new questions, and employs additional sources, especially
the files of the Bombay Government up to 1916 and those of
the Ahmedabad Municipality from 1856.

The research is as complete as I have been able to make it,
but there are lacunae in the sources. Regrettably, there has so
far been little sociological work on Gujarat urban society for
the historian to draw on. There is little statistical data on trade

and production for the nineteenth century; it was not available for the years before 1868, even to the author of the Gazetteer in 1879. I could not locate any nineteenth century records of the Commissioner of the Northern Division of the Bombay Presidency and they have presumably been destroyed. The records of the Collector and City Survey Office were burned in 1919 in the riots that followed the reported arrest of Mahatma Gandhi during the agitation over the Rowlatt Act; fortunately they were used in the preparation of the Gazetteer and all matters considered important at the time were, of course, referred to Bombay, where many (but not all) of the records survive.

Anyone who writes on India must grapple with difficult problems of terminology and spelling since usage varies from time to time and place to place. In general, the local forms are used in this book, for example, Vania, not *bania*. The word *saraf* (shroff), is used to denote the indigenous financier or "banker," though other terms in use were *sahukar*, *savakar*, *nanavati*, and *parekh*. The word *seth* denotes the head of a trade-guild, or any big merchant or financier or millowner; and *mahajan* denotes a guild, though elsewhere in India it often means simply a big merchant. Jain has been used to describe people who were more often known in the nineteenth century as *shravak*; and Patidar has been used in most places instead of Kanbi in conformity with present usage, though originally there was a distinction. I hope the reader will be tolerant of any inconsistencies that remain.

CHAPTER I

Old Ahmedabad

Traditional India, under both Hindu and Muslim rulers, was a land of great cities. Despite a persistent anti-urban tone to some of its literature, Hindu civilization had its highest institutional expression in the cities, where many castes met and its "great tradition" was elaborated and refined. The Hindus had elaborate and comprehensive theories of city planning, while the urban bias of Islam, both in West Asia and in India, has often been remarked by scholars. There were many reasons for the existence of Indian cities: there were capitals, ports, and emporia, centres of handicraft production, pilgrim, temple, and monastery cities, educational centres, and garrison cities.[1] Many had more than one function,

[1] For Gujarat, see Altekar, "History of Important Ancient Towns," Majmudar, *Cultural History of Gujarat*, Deshpande, "Cities and Towns of Bombay Province," and Pocock, "Sociologies: Urban and Rural" (III).

as trade, industry, organized religion, and learning followed
the flag. Although some towns and cities, for example Banaras
and Patna, have had a long, continuous existence, the sub-
continent is dotted with the ruins of many others that did not
survive into modern times. Babar, the first of the Mughal emperors, wrote that in India, towns were quickly set up or
abandoned, because the crops were dependent on rain rather
than on elaborate irrigation systems, and building materials
were plentiful.[2] There were other reasons besides the easy
climate for the ephemeral nature of many Indian cities compared to those Babar knew in Central Asia and to European
cities also. There were the whims of rulers, who could, like
Akbar, build a Fatehpur Sikri and then abandon it; there were
the shifting courses of rivers, swollen by monsoon rains, and
the silting up of harbours; there were the countless invasions
and wars, with each new ruler setting up his own capital. The
greatest cities of traditional India, in their time among the
largest in the world, were the capitals of the empires: Patali-
putra, Kanyakubja, Vijayanagar, Delhi, and Agra.

Travellers have left descriptions of some of these cities: the
splendour of the palaces, temples, and mosques, the cosmopolitan bazaars, the squalor in which the common people lived,
and most importantly, the dependence of all on the court.
Thevenot wrote of seventeenth-century Delhi:

> Seeing there is an extraordinary crowd in the streets while
> the Court is there, the Indians are persuaded that it is the
> most populous City in the World; and nevertheless I have
> been told, that it appears to be a Desert when the King is
> absent. This will not seem strange if we consider, that the
> Court of the Great Mogul is very numerous, because the
> great Men of the Empire are almost all there, who have vast
> retinues, because their Servants cost them but little in Diet

[2] Habib, p. 117 (III).

and Cloaths, that that court is attended by above thirty five thousand Horse, and ten or twelve thousand Foot, which may be called an Army, and that every soldier hath his Wife, Children and Servants, who for the most part are married also, and have a great many children as well as their masters. If to these we add all the drudges and rascally people which courts and Armies commonly draw after them, and then the great number of Merchants and other Trading People, who are obliged to stick to them, because in that country there is no Trade nor Money to be got but at Court. When I say, we consider Dehly void of all those I have mentioned, and of many more still, it will easily be believed, that that Town is no great matter when the King is not there; and if there have been four hundred thousand Men in it when he was there, there hardly remains the sixth part in his absence.[3]

When the Emperor left, this host accompanied him as a vast travelling city with a population of hundreds of thousands. When the empire declined, so did the city.

Thevenot's description has been quoted here because it was typical of many important Indian cities, particularly the great political capitals, and because it has often been assumed to have been true of all. But the city of Ahmedabad did not owe its importance just to its being a seat of government; it survived several changes of rulers, and it had more than ephemeral reasons for its existence. This Asian city was not dependent on the whims of a despotic court, nor was it peopled by quivering subjects, too ridden by magical beliefs and divided by caste to show any corporate spirit or economic rationality. It was a city of mixed type, more than a political capital and more than an emporium.

Ahmedabad was founded in 1411 A.D. by Sultan Ahmed Shah of Gujarat, on a site close to the much older trading centre

[3] Sen, pp. 60–61 (III).

of Asaval (or Asapalli or Karnavati). He was ambitious to be
the founder of a great line of kings and he wanted to replace
the old Hindu capital of Anhilvad Patan, 70 miles to the north,
with a capital of his own making. He encouraged merchants,
weavers, and skilled craftsmen to come to Ahmedabad and
make it a flourishing commercial and industrial city as well.
For a hundred years it grew in wealth and splendour, then for
sixty years declined with the decay of the Gujarat dynasty
and Portuguese interference with its trade. In 1572 it became
part of the Mughal Empire, the seat of the Mughal Viceroy
of Gujarat, and its prosperity recovered, but in the eighteenth
century a period of disorder set in with the disintegration of
the Empire. From 1738 to 1753 it was ruled by the Muslims
and Marathas jointly, and in 1757 passed completely into
Maratha hands. In 1817 it was annexed by the East India
Company.

Ahmedabad lies on both banks of the river Sabarmati, fifty
miles from its mouth and 173 feet above mean sea level. Except
in the rainy season, the Sabarmati is a thin stream in a broad bed
of deep sand. The old walled city was on the east bank and
covered an area of two square miles, enclosed within walls
completed in 1487. To the south are the fertile fields of Gujarat,
to the north the deserts of Rajasthan. Ahmedabad was a cross-
roads, commanding the caravan routes to Rajasthan and Delhi
to the north, Malwa to the east, Sind with its port of Tatta
(Lahari Bandar) to the west, and the ports of Cambay, Surat,
and Broach to the south. The Sabarmati is not navigable and
Ahmedabad's exports formerly travelled overland—now by
rail. Ahmedabad's climate is dry and the camels of the desert
still trudge through its streets.

Ahmedabad has always been a wealthy city by Indian standards and its people have a reputation for industry and thrift.
It has always been a textile centre and was once famed for the
cloths which were exported through Cambay, the main port,

to the Persian Gulf and Arabian ports, Southeast Asia, and
other parts of India. Fine velvet, silk, and gold and silver brocades reached the Middle East and Europe. Coarse, brightly
dyed Ahmedabad cottons were worn in Africa and Southeast
Asia. Ships from many countries came to Cambay and the
Dutch and English East India Companies had factors in Ahmedabad to buy indigo, saltpetre, and textiles. Mandelslo
(1638) remarked on the ease with which foreign bills of exchange could be procured in Ahmedabad since the Vanias had
correspondents in places as far away as Constantinople.[4] A
stream of donkeys and camels carried luxury imports from the
West through the warehouses of Ahmedabad to the courts of
Delhi and Agra and Rajasthan and Malwa. Among the products
they brought back were drugs for export and coarse cloth
to be dyed in the city. Nearby Sarkhej was the most important centre of indigo production in western India, and it was
said that the skill of Ahmedabad's dyers was lost when they
were moved far from the city, because of the qualities of the
waters of the Sabarmati and nearby wells. Ahmedabad's Muslim weavers and Hindu and Jain financiers and merchants cooperated to bring great wealth to the city. Ahmedabad had
little religious significance either for Hindus or for Muslims;
it was not a holy city like Kanchipuram, and there were no
important shrines or festivals to attract pilgrims from afar, as
to Banaras. People came to Ahmedabad to do business.

Under the Sultans of Gujarat and Mughal Viceroys, Ahmedabad was a splendid city by the standards of the time. Before the rise of Mughal Agra and Delhi it was probably the
finest in India. The Muslim historian Firishtah wrote, "It is
hardly necessary to add that this is, on the whole, the hand-
somest city in Hindoostan, and perhaps in the world."[5] Most

[4] M. S. Commissariat, *Mandelslo's Travels*, p. 28 (III).
[5] Mahomed Kasim Firishtah, IV, 14 (III).

of the houses were built of brick and mortar, the roofs were
tiled, and the main streets could take ten carriages abreast. Cesar
Fredericke, a merchant of Venice, thought it very well made
for a city of the "gentiles," and he was astonished by the extent
of the trade of Cambay.[6] Visitors remarked on the beauty of
Ahmedabad's stone buildings, in "the most Hindu of Indo-
Saracenic styles," much influenced by the Jain architecture of
medieval Gujarat. Ahmedabad's mosques and tombs are unpre-
tentious in size, but the rich detail, the delicate tracery, and
ornamented minarets make them most distinctive and more
Indian in feeling than Muslim architecture elsewhere in India.
Pillars were taken from old Hindu buildings in Anhilvad Patan
and elsewhere, and Hindu and Jain craftsmen were employed.
Visitors noted, too, the wide streets lined with tall trees, and
the many garden suburbs, for Ahmedabad was a spacious city
in those days.[7]

The great public buildings were Muslim mosques and
tombs (in which Ahmedabad is one of the most richly endowed cities in India), but the tone of the city was as much
Hindu as Muslim. Perhaps it is not without significance that
the most famous motif of Ahmedabad's architecture is the
banyan tree strangling the palm. It is surely not true, as sometimes has been stated, that the Hindus were once confined to
the suburbs, though it is possible that the Bhadra citadel area
was once reserved for the Muslim rulers. Until the time of
the Marathas, the officers of state were largely Muslim and
the skilled weavers were Muslims. But the financiers and
traders were generally Hindus and Jains, except for the Bohoras, who traded in silk and piece goods. The wealth of Ahmedabad was controlled by Hindus and Jains, especially the
old, established family firms. These constituted a plutocracy

[6] Forbes, III, 86 (III).
[7] *Ahmedabad Gazetteer* (*Gazetteer of the Bombay Presidency*, Vol.
IV), pp. 249–266 (II).

which was largely hereditary (for, unlike that of the officials, there was no escheat of merchants' property). The well established and highly respectable sarafi families (often loosely called "bankers," though they used their own capital in the main, rather than deposits) dealt in each other's *hundis* (cheques for payments over distances), changed coins, acted as army paymasters and financiers to princes and merchants and as farmers of the land revenue and tolls, provided insurance, served as trustees for religious and charitable purposes, and sometimes engaged in commercial activities on their own account.

In the time of the Mughal emperors Jahangir, Shah Jahan, and Aurangzeb, the head of the Jain community was the court jeweller and financier, Shantidas Jawahari, who helped to provide for the needs of the luxurious courts at Agra and Delhi. His descendants, who include the leading millowner of Ahmedabad, still have a number of orders issued by various rulers in his favour. "Without any connection with the nobility of the Mughal Empire, Shantidas was able to exercise, by virtue of his business connections and his vast riches, an influence at the court of successive Mughal Emperors from the time of Jahangir to the succession of Aurangzeb which must have been envied by many an exalted *amir* or *mansabdar* of the Empire."[8] He was able to persuade Shah Jahan to order his young and excessively orthodox son, Aurangzeb, who was appointed Viceroy of Gujarat in 1645, to return a Jain temple which he had converted into a mosque and to make restitution for the damage he had done to it. When Shah Jahan died, Prince Murad took 550,000 rupees from the sons of Shantidas in order to fight for the succession. When Aurangzeb defeated Murad he had the money repaid and instructed his officers not to obstruct the affairs of Shantidas or the inhabitants of Ahmed-

[8] M. S. Commissariat, *Studies in the History of Gujarat*, p. 53 (III).

abad, thus demonstrating his recognition of the importance of financiers like Shantidas and his desire to win their support.[9]

The merchants and financiers of the Mughal Empire had an important place in the complex social and political system of the day. They ranged from the humble village shopkeeper and money-lender to the millionaire financier, and their power, prestige, and wealth varied from village to city and from region to region. It is true that nowhere did they have prestige if they did not have wealth, as Brahmins often did, but wealth usually conferred secular prestige. There was no real division of interest between the merchants and financiers and the military, official class of the empire. The former provided the luxury goods the latter needed, and in a system which was never as bureaucratic in practice as Akbar and Todar Mal would have preferred, they assisted in the collection of taxes, whether in kind or in cash, and in their transmission from village to capital and to the armies in the field. The Vanias of Ahmedabad throve on Mughal peace and order and their services contributed much to ensure the prosperity of the empire. Indeed, such was the social position, corporate spirit, enterprise, and economic sophistication of the mercantile elite of Ahmedabad that one may well wonder (with more justification than of other areas of India, which provide a greater contrast with Western Europe) why it was able to achieve its full potential only under British rule. The answer to this question is perhaps less likely to be found, if it is to be found at all, in the sociology of religion than in economics and politics—in factors such as the nature and size of the market and labour supply and the absence of competition, which provided little incentive to innovate or question established social relationships, in the rule of a military elite not principally dependent on revenue from commerce, and in political turbulence.

[9] M. S. Commissariat, "Imperial Mughal Farmans in Gujarat"; Ali Muhammad Khan, pp. 210–212 (III).

The influence of the financiers and merchants of Ahmedabad appeared in the survival there of certain old institutions of
Hindu mercantile cities: the mahajans and the Nagarseth.
Whereas in other parts of India the guilds, so powerful in the
time of the Buddha and for centuries afterwards, had all but
disappeared, squeezed between royal and caste power, they
were still important in the nineteenth century in Gujarat, and
to a lesser extent in Rajasthan, and traces of them were to be
found as far east as Banaras and as far south as Poona.[10] In Ahmedabad they are by no means unimportant even now. In pre-
Mughal and Mughal days, they were as much rulers of the city
as the royal governors and officials and for the individual of
far more immediate significance.

The centre of the royal government of the city was its
citadel, the Bhadra fort (named after a similar fort at Anhilvad
Patan dedicated to Bhadra Kali, the goddess Kali in her aus-
picious form, and, incidentally, the patron goddess of Ahmedabad). In Mughal times the city was under the Subahdar
(Governor) of Gujarat and was not self-governing in the
sense that European cities were self-governing. The Subahdar
was responsible for the defence of the city, criminal justice
and the police, and the Diwan for finance. Among the important subordinate officials were the Faujdars or chiefs of
police in the neighbourhood of Ahmedabad, the Kazis, who
administered both civil and criminal law, and the Kotwal,
who was head of the city's police. The Kotwal's duties included the watch and ward of the city, the regulation of the
market (including the prevention of monopolies, over-
pricing, and short weights), the care and legitimate disposal
of heirless property, the prevention of social abuses such as

[10] For the mahajans and Nagarseth elsewhere, see Gadgil, *Origins of
the Modern Indian Business Class*, pp. 23–28. For the Nagarseth and
urban government in ancient times, see Kane, III, 178–183. For the Gujarat mercantile situation, see Lamb, "The Indian Merchant." For
Gujarat castes, see Enthoven, *The Tribes and Castes of Bombay* (III).

fickle monsoon rains were late, he would circumambulate the city walls, pouring milk on the ground to appease Indra. Doubtless there were many occasions when his prestige and influence contributed to the settling of quarrels between mahajans or individuals or in interceding with the royal officials.[15] Similarly, there were the Kazis to speak for the Muslim community. The office of chief Kazi has been hereditary in one family for over 400 years.[16] The Kazi was not simply a servant of the Subahdar, but like the Nagarseth, a buffer between the government and the communities within the city.

The Nagarseth family are Oswal Jains. This reflects the great importance of the Jain community in Ahmedabad. At the census of 1872, they comprised 10.03% of the population and formed one of its richest communities.[17] The Vania castes of Rajasthan and Gujarat remained strongholds of Jainism when it largely died out elsewhere after the days of the great Jain communities of medieval India. The prevailing vegetarianism in Ahmedabad, and its tenderness towards the animal kingdom, are Jain legacies. Whether there is a causal relationship between business success and Jainism is an even more controversial matter than the famous debate over the connection between Protestantism and capitalism. But just as rapid economic growth has taken place in many societies that are not Protestant, so the Jains are not the only businessmen of Gujarat. It is just as likely that they were influenced by the general environment favourable to business enterprise as the Parsis were by the same environment. Similarly, the Jain Marwaris of Rajasthan come from an infertile country crossed by trade routes, and their business success in modern India derives more from this circumstance, and from the contraction of local opportunities in trade and the financing of princely wars, than from their re-

---

[15] *Ahmedabad Gazetteer*, pp. 113–114 (II).
[16] Petition of Mahomed Hoossein Oodean, R.D. 196/1845 (I).
[17] *Ahmedabad Gazetteer*, p. 293 (II).

ligion. In the Karnatak, the Jains are largely illiterate agriculturists. It is true, however, that the Ahmedabad Jains were more
prosperous as a community and better educated than their
Vaishnava fellow Vanias. Nor can it be denied that Jainism has
helped to mould the character of the Gujarati Vanias, but so
too has Vaishnavism.

There were about forty guilds in Ahmedabad. These were
predominantly Hindu or Jain bodies. The Muslim guilds were
in "weak imitation of Hindu models"[18] and not comparable
with the guilds which were so important in Islamic cities in
the middle east. The guilds of merchants and financiers were
known as *mahajans* and their hereditary heads as *seths*. Among
them the most important were the sarafs' mahajan, the cloth
dealers' mahajan, and the raw silk dealers' mahajan. The artisan
guilds were known as *panch* and their heads as *patels*. A guild
could embrace members of several castes, and a caste members of several guilds; in some cases they were coterminous.
There was no strict separation of religious, social, and occupational problems. Admission to a guild was hereditary or by
purchase. Expulsion was an occupational and often a social
disaster. The guilds controlled admissions, restricted competition, maintained joint charities through levies on their members, kept up standards, determined wages, controlled prices
(sometimes), set holidays, and safeguarded the interests of their
members against the government, other guilds, and outsiders.
The mahajans were able to exclude foreigners from the commerce of Ahmedabad and to tame social conflicts within the
city. It is true that they could act as a brake upon innovation
and improvement and Andrew Dunlop, the first Collector of
Ahmedabad, deplored this, but in the traditional situation
their advantages were more obvious.

The relationship between the institutions of sect, caste,

18 Hopkins, p. 178 (III).

guild, and Nagarseth, was complex. There was no clear differentiation among the various roles. For instance, the Nagarseth
was head of the sarafs' guild and head of the Jain community,
and he also spoke for the city as a whole, while he owed his
position to the wealth, charities, and public spirit of his family
over several generations. The head of the cloth-dealers' mahajan was sometimes called *chautano seth* (market chief) and
he was also looked upon as the head of the Vaishnava sect. The
two would consult together on important public matters. Yet
both sarafs and cloth-dealers could be either Jains or Vaishnavas, and inevitably there was confusion of sectarian and commercial interests. The Jains, for example, collected funds from
the cloth-dealers' mahajan for the support of their *panjarapol*
(animal home). Similarly, penalties for breaches of caste rules
could be enforced by a guild composed of several castes, even
more so by those where caste and guild were coterminous; for
instance, a Visa Shrimali Vania was expelled from the cloth
dealers' mahajan, and thus compelled to leave Ahmedabad to
make a living, because he married a widow.[19]

As in other traditional cities, the social divisions of the
population were reflected in the layout of the city. In old
Ahmedabad there was less differentiation of working and living quarters than in the modern city. Most people worked at
home, except when they went to market to sell their wares. The
chief markets were the Friday fair (in the Maidan Shahi, the
space between the Bhadra fort and the Tin Darwaza—three
gates, as the people gathered for the Friday prayers in the Jama
Masjid—great mosque), the Manek Chowk, and the market
centres near the main gates. The size of most industrial or
commercial undertakings did not warrant the employment of
large groups of people outside the family. Exceptions were the
paper factories and the silk industry, with its many complicated

[19] For the mahajans and Nagarseth of Ahmedabad, see Hopkins, and
Ratnamanirao, pp. 545–562 (III), and *Ahmedabad Gazetteer*, pp. 106–
116 (II).

processes, each demanding specialized skills; and the offices of the government with their armies of clerks, for the ponderous bureaucracy of modern India predates even the British period. But most people lived and worked in a housegroup known as a *pol*, normally (but not invariably) associated with one caste.

These pols, of which there were 356 in 1872, are still among the curiosities of India. They comprise a labyrinth of high wooden houses, streets too narrow for wheeled traffic, and cul-de-sacs. A pol would have only one, or at the most two entrances (apart from secret ones), one main street with crooked lanes branching on either side, and walls and gates (now removed) which were barred at night. There was often a quadrangle, with a temple and well, and there were common latrines at the entrance. To some extent the house property in the pol was held in common. This was the situation in 1879:

> Formerly no man could sell or mortgage a house to an outsider without first offering it to the people of the pol. Though this rule is not now kept, inmates of a pol are careful to sell to men of their own class and never to people of low caste. When a house is mortgaged or sold, the people of the pol have a right to claim from one-half to two per cent of the money received. Again, on wedding and other great family occasions, each householder is expected to feast the whole pol, and in some cases all the men of the pol, though not of the same caste, are expected to attend any funeral that may take place. If the pol rules are slighted, the offender is fined, and, in former times, till he paid, he was not allowed to light a lamp in his house or to give a feast. The money gathered from gifts, fines, and the percentage on house property sales forms a common fund managed by the leaders, seths, of the pol. This is spent on repairs to the pol gate, the pol privies, or the pol well.[20]

The lanes were shaded by multi-storied wooden houses, with

[20] *Ahmedabad Gazetteer*, p. 295 (II).

carved, unpainted fronts, and eaves that almost met across the
lanes. In 1903 Forrest wrote, "Nowhere does one feel oneself
more thoroughly in an eastern city of past times than in the
narrow streets of Ahmedabad, thick with ancient houses, none
so poor as not to have a doorway or a window or a wooden
pillar carved finely."[21] The pols provided privacy to a group
and warm or oppressive cosiness to an individual impossible in
a modern city. There was, too, no differentiation of area of
residence by wealth. The rich seths of Ahmedabad lived in
the pols among their caste fellows, rich and poor alike, not as
they do today, in surburban bungalows surrounded by spacious
grounds.

In the days of Mughal rule, before the decline of Ahmedabad, there were many *puras* (suburbs) outside the walled
city. Those on the other bank were connected with the city
by ford in the dry weather or by boat. These puras were not
dormitory suburbs for those who worked in the city, as are
their modern equivalents on the same sites, but were the seats
of Mughal officers. They were surrounded by gardens and
were peopled by all those who served and followed the rich
and powerful. They were miniature cities, owing their existence to the presence of the rulers; and when the rulers left,
their puras died, leaving only isolated tombs and mosques and
mounds of bricks, once fine walls or palaces. The palaces of
the nobles used to extend from the present Ellis Bridge to
Sarkhej. But some of the puras were founded by merchants
and were extensions of the economic life of the main city of
Ahmedabad. The suburb of Madhavpura, for instance, was
founded by the Nagarseth's family in Maratha times. They
built a square, surrounded by shops and warehouses, and were
granted the right to levy dues on the cartmen who brought
their goods to sell in this secure market place. Again, because
the suburb of Raghunathpura "was in a ruinous state and

[21] Forrest, p. 72 (III).

Vukhutchund Seth has been the means of causing the same Poora to be inhabited," he was granted, again under the Marathas, the right to collect dues on the carts of grain and the cattle brought through the suburb.[22]

It is said that Ahmedabad used to hang on three threads: gold, silk, and cotton. It was for her silk manufactures that she was chiefly famed, especially for the bright colours of the plain silks, and the durability and non-fading qualities of the brocades with patterns woven of gold and silver thread. Raw silk was imported from Bengal, China, and Central Asia. The manufacture was a complex process; from the imported raw silk to the final product there were eleven separate sets of workmen. The raw silk was imported by merchants called *tagias*, while other merchants would pay the workmen and export the finished product. Generally the workmen lived in their own houses, though there were workshops also, including, in Mughal times, state *karkhanas*. Cotton spinning and the weaving, dyeing, and printing of cotton cloth were also important industries. Ahmedabad's cotton cloth was not noted for its fineness but for its strength and fast bright colours. Other important manufactures were high-quality paper and woodwork. Of the goods which passed through the city and brought profits to its merchants, drugs and indigo were especially important.

Ahmedabad's fortunes were bound up with a wide area and the city provided a livelihood for many people outside it. There was its immediate hinterland which supplied raw cotton and food, and wood for houses, carts, and fuel. The Ahmedabad market in food grains was particularly important for the development of the fertile Kaira district and her tough and enterprising Lewa Patidar caste of peasant proprietors. The agricultural areas around Ahmedabad also provided tax reve-

[22] Survey of suburbs, G.D. 72/1901; quotation from sanad of 1757, G.D. 308/1834 (I).

nues for the support of the government and new residents for
the city. Like other pre-modern cities, Ahmedabad could not
replenish its population without immigration from the rural
areas. The excess of deaths over births was counteracted by
the drift to the city of some of the more enterprising of the
rural population, or deviants, misfits, and the curious. Many
of these brought their families to the city or sent for them subsequently. In 1872 there were 58,477 males and 58,396 females
in Ahmedabad, an equality of the sexes which one British authority thought remarkable for an Indian city.[23] The population of Ahmedabad was essentially a rooted urban population,
and was not made up of a large number of floating individuals.
Few agriculturists lived in the city.

There was, however, a close connection between the
city and the countryside. The Vanias of Ahmedabad played
an important part in the process of converting the produce of
the peasantry of the surrounding areas into tax revenues. Some
of those entitled to receive a share in the produce of the soil—
the proprietors of *taluqdari* villages—lived in the city. Many of
the peasants were in debt to money-lenders and petty traders,
who in 1825 were said to keep them in a state of "interminable
dependence," and these borrowed, in their turn, from the larger
firms in the city.[24] Cloth woven in the villages by Muslims and
Dheds was dyed in the city, and some of the preliminary stages
of silk manufacture such as reeling and spinning were carried
out in the adjacent villages, chiefly by Patidars in their spare

[23] Dr. Hewlett's report, G.D. 78/1875 (I). In 1847 there were, according to British figures, 1,717 births (1.25%) and 3,815 deaths (4%) in
Ahmedabad city, as against 19,615 births (3.25%) and 17,918 deaths
(2.75%) in Ahmedabad district as a whole. (Fawcett, p. 69) (II). But
the excess of recorded deaths over recorded births among Ahmedabadi
residents was due in part to the better facilities for recording deaths (the
bodies passed through the city gates), plus the fact that many women
went to their home villages for childbirth. (Fernandez, Report on
Municipality, 9 Aug. 1882, G.D. 10/1883) (I).

[24] Cruikshank, p. 122 (II).

time. There was no mass market in the villages for the city's
manufactures as most of the people wore coarse homespun
cloth. But some of the richer people in the countryside sought
luxury articles made in the city, and other villagers did buy
articles when they came to the Friday fair to sell their agricultural produce and cloth. Ahmedabad did not have the parasitic,
exploitative relationship to the surrounding countryside so
often assumed to have been true of Asian cities in general, but
was more like traditional European commercial and industrial
cities.

From the second quarter of the seventeenth century,
Ahmedabad fell into the decline from which it was rescued by
British rule and modern industry. The population fell from
perhaps between a quarter and a half million at the peak of the
city's greatness to about 80,000 when the British arrived in
1817. Aurangzeb's prolonged stay in the Deccan, the decline
of the Mughal Empire and the resulting shift of India's political centre of gravity towards the south and east weakened Ahmedabad's importance as a centre of trade. But there were
other reasons for the decline of the city. Ahmedabad's sea-
borne exports through Cambay were falling off. Contemporaries blamed the piracy of the European intruders in Asian
waters; the Gulf of Cambay could be easily blockaded and
the Portuguese controlled its entrance from Diu and Daman.
India's own shipping was being supplanted by that of foreigners. Another important reason was the silting of the mouth
of the river Mahi, which has, over the years, turned Cambay
into an insignificant and unsuitable port.[25] Surat, which first
came into prominence in the seventeenth century as a port for
the pilgrim traffic to Mecca, was a new rival to Ahmedabad and
Cambay as a centre of trade, and was given even greater im-

[25] *Ahmedabad Gazetteer*, pp. 251–257, and *Cambay Gazetteer*, pp.
219–220 (II).

portance when the European companies established their factories there. Ahmedabad's supremacy in textile exports was
challenged by other manufacturers in Sind, the Punjab, and
the Gangetic plain. Samples of Gujarat fabrics were sent to the
Coromandel Coast and manufacture was stimulated there by
the agents of the Europeans companies. The terrible famine
which depopulated Gujarat in 1630–32 was followed by a
decline in the standards and rise in the price of Gujarat textiles
and helped to turn European eyes to these other areas. From
this time onward, Ahmedabad tended to specialize in luxury
fabrics rather than in the cheaper varieties.[26]

Beyond its immediate hinterland, Ahmedabad was also
affected by events over a large part of northern, western, and
central India. The degree of political control which could be
exercised over Gujarat determined the collection of land revenue. This revenue, through the spending of the official class in
Ahmedabad, affected the elegance and much of the prosperity
of the city. A good return from the land revenue also ensured
that commerce would not be crippled by ruinous taxes and
tolls imposed through fiscal desperation. The extent of political control also affected the security of the caravan routes into
Rajasthan, Malwa, and Sind. When control weakened in the
eighteenth century, the commerce of Ahmedabad declined.
But wider causes were operating also. The chronic warfare of
that century, the decay of urban life elsewhere from the standards of luxurious spending appropriate to a more settled age,
the insecurity of the roads, and the exactions of every petty
chieftain and princeling whose territory was traversed by the
caravans reduced the demand for Ahmedabad's products. The
decline of Mughal power and the rise of successor States, including those of the Marathas, did enable rich financiers like

[26] Irwin, "Indian Textile Trade in the Seventeenth Century" (III).

the Jagat Seths of Murshidabad, the Arjunji Nathjis of Surat, and the various sarafs to whom the Gaikwads of Baroda were indebted, to exercise considerable political influence; but its overall effect on Indian trade and production was unfavourable.

The political decline of Ahmedabad was chronicled by Ali Muhammad Khan in his *Mirat-i-Ahmadi*. He tells of disputes between the Muslim and Rajput officers, attempts to ward off the Marathas and Kolis, communal rioting and merchants' armed retainers, depopulation of the city and suburbs, extortion, depreciation of the currency, and the temporary imprisonment of successive Nagarseths. It is clear that the decline and misgovernment often blamed on the Marathas had begun before they took over. The preceding Rajput officers emerge from the chronicle in a most unfavourable light. But if Maratha rule was far from being the only reason for Ahmedabad's decline, still it was an important one, and little good is said, or indeed can be said, of the Marathas as rulers of the city. It is true that they did not pillage the mosques, that they continued to patronize Muslim as well as Hindu holiness and learning, and that they did not ride roughshod over traditional usages, except where financial matters were involved. But their administrative system was not equal to the task of governing a great commercial city like Ahmedabad, nor did their financial troubles permit them to regard it as more than a source of aggrandizement. In fact, they paid more constructive attention to Patan, where they built a wall, than to Ahmedabad. Under the Peshwas, Poona, on the arid Deccan, became a metropolis, drawing Gujarati and Marwari financiers and merchants to the south. "After the Mahrattas conquered Gujarat, the weavers of keemcabs and other rich stuff, the embroiderers, jewellers, painters, and inlayers of ivory, ebony, and sandal-wood, meeting with no encouragement from the Mahratta government emigrated from Ahmedabad to Surat, and other flourishing cities in the

western districts of Hindostan, where they have resumed their
employment with great success."[27] Others went to Patan and
Banaras. The former Mughal officers and many other Muslims
of high birth left to find service with other princes or offered
themselves as soldiers of fortune. Ahmedabad became a source
of profit to successive Maratha governors, while the Peshwas
and the Gaikwads competed to wring what they could from
it. The situation was better at some times than at others: the
period of sole control by the Gaikwad between 1800 and 1814
was less burdensome to the city that the periods when the
administration and taxation of the city were divided between
the Peshwa and the Gaikwad, or usurped by Abu Shelukar, the
Peshwa's governor, 1798–1800, whose rule is a byword in
Ahmedabad for oppression and cruelty. Illegal exactions vied
with legal ones and those who were not quick enough to bribe
the Maratha officers, or their local stooges, were beaten and tor-
tured.

   Forbes described Ahmedabad as he saw it in 1781 when he
accompanied a Maratha-British army on its campaign: "Soli-
tude, poverty, and desolation. You behold the most heterogene-
ous mixture of Mogul splendour and Mahratta barbarism; a
noble cupola, overshadowing hovels of mud; small windows,
ill-fashioned doors, and dirty cells introduced under a superb
portico; a marble corridore filled up with choolas, or cooking
places, composed of mud, cow-dung, and unburnt bricks."[28]
He compared Ahmedabad to Nineveh and Babylon and reflected that until then he had had no idea of the extent of
oriental magnificence. He thought the city doomed never to
recover. The suburbs were deserted. The walls had not been
repaired and tigers were occasionally seen within them. The
people huddled together for protection. With the connivance

[27] Forbes, I, 257–258 (III).
[28] Forbes, III, 120 (III).

or indifference of the Maratha officers, building restrictions had been disregarded and streets narrowed or even blocked.

Ahmedabad's industry, trade, and finance contracted but still they survived. The Marathas had only a small native commercial and financial class and their Kunbi leaders in Gujarat were glad to use the Gujarati sarafs, even in preference to their own Brahmin administrators, of whom they were often jealous. The Marathas displaced the old Muslim elite but did not fully replace it with their own. This gave opportunities to local groups, like the Patidars of Kaira and the sarafs of Ahmedabad. The sarafs advanced money to the rulers on the security of the land revenue, which they helped to collect. The vast Maratha armies, no longer bands of marauding horsemen living off the land, had to be fed and paid, even in arrears. Revenue had to be transferred over long distances to Poona. Allies had to be subsidised. The sarafs of Ahmedabad established agencies at Baroda, Poona, and elsewhere. They followed the revenue-collecting forces on their tours. In the field, they paid the troops on the security of their commanders, charging a small discount, and were reimbursed by the state treasury on presenting the commanders' receipts. The Maratha officers were no longer as indifferent to comfort as their hardy forbears. Forbes wrote that the Marathas preferred camps and tents to cities and houses but their camps were now great travelling cities like those of the Mughals. He described a Maratha camp with its bazaar, containing thousands of tents where trades and professions were carried on with as much regularity as in a city. There were goldsmiths, jewellers, bankers, drapers, druggists, cooks, confectioners, carpenters, tailors, tent-washers, corn-grinders, farriers, silver, iron and coppersmiths, all with their wives and children.[29] Among them were Ahmedabadis. When a Maratha officer transferred money he did so through a Gujarati saraf.

[29] Forbes, II, 44–54 (III).

He bought his precious stones from a Gujarati jeweller. His
fine coat was of Ahmedabad *kinkhab* (brocade worked with
gold and silver thread). And not all the profits flowed back into
the Maratha coffers. There were still rich men in Ahmedabad.

The people of Gujarat still invested Ahmedabad with the
prestige that its position as a centre of elegance and grandeur
and power had earned it over the centuries. One of the reasons
advanced in 1817 by Carnac, the British Resident at Baroda, in
urging the British annexation was the symbolic value of the
city as the traditional seat of government in Gujarat:

> The veneration in which it is held by the country at large
> renders the power possessing it, by the operation of such in-
> fluence, capable of preserving the peace of the province with-
> out having resort to extraordinary means for the purpose.
> The Peninsula of Kattywar has been accustomed to look to
> Ahmedabad as the seat of authority, and its fame is superior
> to that of any city on the western side of India . . .

> Subject to the mild and paternal Government of the Honour-
> able Company, this beautiful city would again resume its
> importance and the prospects of happiness be joyfully hailed
> in a change of master. It is not easy to enumerate the variety
> of its riches and beauty in former times or to describe its
> present comparative impoverished appearance by the means
> of bad government but even in its adversity, the manufac-
> ures are not surpassed in elegance and the bounty of nature
> yet fixes its superior pretensions to admiration. Under the
> administration of British laws which protect property and
> encourage every exertion of lucrative industry, the extensive
> merchandise for which Ahmedabad was once distinguished
> would become renewed to the diffusion of many blessings
> over the Province in Guzerat—in a word, it may not be haz-
> arding too much to say, that the city of Ahmedabad placed
> in the hands of the British Government promises to prove

a source not only of great Revenue, but a possession worthy
of a splendid and enlightened nation.[30]

Ahmedabad's economy was eclipsed but her prestige as the first
city of Gujarat was still intact and so was the social structure of
her resilient and tough people.

The spirit of Ahmedabad is utilitarian and materialistic.
In the study which he published in 1929, Ratnamanirao remarked on the lack of interest in the arts and graces of life.[31]
In contrast to Surat, Ahmedabad followed Kubera, the hard
god of wealth, not Lakshmi, whose wealth is softened by
beauty and pleasure. Perhaps Lakshmi ceded first place to Kubera during the troubled eighteenth century and is only now
returning. What sort of person was the Ahmedabadi of the
mercantile castes? He evolved during centuries of life in a
flourishing industrial and commercial city, with its strong mahajan traditions, and withstood nearly a century of regression
and misrule. All oral and written accounts present a stereotype
of him which goes like this.[32] He was industrious, shrewd,
practical, patient, self-reliant but co-operative, and thrifty at
home but charitable. He was austere and matter-of-fact and had
simple manners and a quiet dignity. He was not excitable, vain,
or quarrelsome, but if a dispute did arise, he would try to bring
about a peaceful compromise so that work could proceed. He
was adept at not committing himself in advance, at knocking
down a price, and at wriggling out of uncomfortable positions,
but scrupulously honest once he had made a bargain. He was
normally calculating and unimpetuous, but his desire for money
could lead him into speculation, a fault which has lost more

[30] Resident Baroda to Bombay, 26 Aug. 1817, S.D. 301/1817 (I).

[31] Ratnamanirao, *Gujaratnu Patnagar—Amdavad*, pp. 386–389 (III).

[32] Can one really document this? I follow Ratnamanirao, Yashodhar
Mehta, Lobo, and oral evidence.

fortunes in the city than extravagance ever has. With all the
so-called Puritan virtues, he was well suited to the new industrial age and he had a talent for survival which would serve
him well.

CHAPTER II

Under British Rule

By the time the British came to Ahmedabad, the industrial invasion had already brought ruin to several important Indian cities. Bishop Heber had observed this as early as 1824, and in 1840 R. Montgomery Martin, giving evidence before the House of Commons, spoke of the "decay and destruction of Surat, of Dacca, of Murshidabad, and other places where native manufactures have been carried on."[1] His words have been echoed in many histories of India. For comparison with Ahmedabad, let us take these three cities which a century before had been larger and more famous, just as wealthy, and even more important as commercial centres. Ahmedabad survived as a great city and adapted to the new age as they did

[1] Heber, I, 140–141; II, 175 (III). *P.P. 1840*, VIII, 275 (II).

not. The explanation of this difference will be sought both in
the native character of the cities concerned and in the nature
of the Western intrusion and its timing.

In 1700 Murshidabad was selected by Murshid Kuli Khan
as his capital so that he could more effectively control the
territory under his administration and the trade which was
flowing to the European factories in Bengal, including those
at nearby Kasimbazar. It became a populous city with many
rich merchants and many crafts still famous in Bengal, particularly silk and ivory manufacture, but it was never a splendid
capital like Delhi or Agra—or Ahmedabad. It was described by
Mrs. Kindersley in 1766 as a "vile dirty place" and by Hamilton
in 1828 as mostly "a vast assemblage of mud and straw huts,"
and as "the meanest capital in Hindustan."[2] It had no traditions,
no buildings of any distinction, and no one to owe it loyalty.
Its important financiers and traders were the immigrant Marwaris, of whom the most famous was the house of Jagat Seth,
the "Rothschilds of the East," the state bankers and king
makers of Bengal. Once political power in Bengal passed to
the East India Company and the revenue offices were transferred to Calcutta in 1772, Murshidabad lost all reason for being
and fell into rapid decline. It was soon deserted by its grandees
and merchants, some of whom became landed proprietors. It
is now an insignificant place.[3] There have been many cities in
Indian history like Murshidabad.

Dacca, on the other hand, was a great centre of textile
production like Ahmedabad. It had been a Mughal frontier
town and the seat of the governor of Bengal from 1612 to 1700.
Even after the capital was transferred to Murshidabad, Dacca
remained an important centre of trade and industry. In the city
itself and in the surrounding countryside, tens of thousands of

[2] O'Malley, p. 207 (III).
[3] See Hunter, O'Malley, Walsh, and N. K. Sinha, Vol. II, 228–229
(III).

weavers produced fine muslins for export to countries as distant as Southeast Asia and England. This industry had been greatly stimulated, though not of course created, by the demands of the European companies. The fortunes of Dacca depended primarily on the market for her products, not on political events. After England's industrial revolution, machines could produce fine cotton cloth more cheaply than it could be made by hand (if not as well in the best grades) and the contemporaneous Napoleonic wars interrupted the re-export trade in Indian textiles to the Continent. Although the effects of British competition on the Indian handicraft industries have often been exaggerated, their effects on Dacca, which produced muslins for export, are clear enough. Its manufacturing industry was ruined. In 1787 the export of muslins to England was valued at 3,000,000 rupees, in 1807 at 850,000, in 1813 at 350,000, and in 1817 it stopped altogether.[4] The city declined rapidly, though it later revived to some extent as a district headquarters and then as a provincial capital. Today it is the capital of East Pakistan and, freed from the competition of Calcutta, is again an industrial centre.

Surat, the third city taken for comparison, was a very old trade centre like most of the cities of Gujarat, where the rivers have relatively stable courses compared to Bengal. In the seventeenth century it became prominent as a port for the pilgrims going to Mecca and for the European trading companies. Some of its merchants became very rich, among them the famous monopolist, Virji Vora, in the seventeenth century, and the Arjunji Nathjis in the late eighteenth and early nineteenth centuries, who helped finance the armies of the East India Company.[5] But by then Surat was in decline: its harbour was silting up, and even more important (since it could use Swally Roads)

[4] Taylor, p. 365 (III). See also N. K. Sinha, Vol. II, 227–228, and A. H. Dani, *Dacca* (III).

[5] N. C. Sinha, pp. 20–21 (III).

was the rise of nearby Bombay, with its English rule, business
connections, and security for commerce and industry in the
turbulent eighteenth century. Surat was too close to Bombay,
too exposed to English competition, to survive as a great city.[6]
Many merchants and artisans left for Bombay, which, under
the lead of the rising Parsi community, became the most West-
ernized and modern city of India. In 1837 Surat was devastated
by a great fire and a flood and by 1839 was said to be the most
declining city in Gujarat, as Ahmedabad was the most flourishing (though the contrast was by no means so marked later in
the century).[7]

In summary, Murshidabad fell because it was a creature of
the court, Dacca because of its dependence on the export trade
and on a single staple which was ousted by a cheaper product,
and Surat because it was both too dependent on overseas commerce (as Ahmedabad was not) and too close to Bombay. We
have already seen that Ahmedabad was a city with a corporate
spirit and an economic life not wholly dependent on a single
court. This chapter will consider, among other things, the
nature of the British challenge to Ahmedabad's commerce and
industry and the geographical advantages it enjoyed. But first
let us examine the circumstances and immediate results of the
British annexation.

Ahmedabad came under British rule in 1817 by treaty
with the Peshwa at Poona and the Gaikwad of Baroda after
the last Maratha War. The Peshwa and Gaikwad had been sharing the revenue from the city. Between 1800 and 1814, on the
persuasion of Sindia and the British, who had their own financial and political reasons, the Peshwa had leased his share of
the revenue to the Gaikwad for an annual payment of 500,000
rupees. With his revenues went his share in the administration

6 Deshpande, p. 281 (III).
7 Minute by L. R. Reid (Acting Chief Sec.) R.D. 133/1217/1840,
p. 174 (I).

of the city. The Gaikwad was allied to the East India Company, which influenced much of the government of the Baroda State, and under this fairly competent administration, the city recovered some of its prosperity, until 1812 and 1813, when it was visited by terrible famine and pestilence. When the lease expired in 1814, the Peshwa refused to renew it because he wanted to preserve his position in Gujarat and to extract more money from the city than he was receiving from the Gaikwad. His advisers also planned to benefit personally from the resumption of the administration. Three years of divided rule and exactions by the Peshwa's officers followed. But in 1817, under the Treaty of Poona, the defeated Peshwa agreed to let his share of the revenues and administration of Ahmedabad to the Gaikwad in perpetuity, and later by separate agreements the Gaikwad, in his turn, agreed to give up all his rights in the city and surrounding countryside to the East India Company in return for an augmented subsidiary force of Company troops and some territory near Baroda. The justification of this British annexation of Ahmedabad was the financial embarrassment of the Gaikwad, who was heavily indebted to numerous sarafs and unable to meet the cost of the subsidiary force. The Bombay Government would have preferred territory in Kathiawar instead, but the Gaikwad was unwilling. The British Resident at Baroda, however, placed great value on the annexation of Ahmedabad because of its political importance and "the commanding influence which the sovereignty over the city of Ahmedabad confers on its possessor in the estimation of the country at large."[8] The Peshwa and the Gaikwad were reluctant to yield the city to the British, not just for financial reasons but for political and sentimental ones also. The Gaikwad and his officers were also strongly opposed to the handing over of his *haveli* (fort in the south-west corner of the city) and the

[8] Resident Baroda to Bombay, 1 Oct. 1817, S.D. 301/1817, p. 1542 (I).

Daskroi (land around the city), having a "superstitious dread" of losing every vestige of authority over a city with such a splendid past.[9] The British insisted on having full authority, and in a supplemental exchange in 1818 the Gaikwad parted with the Daskroi and haveli.

When John Andrew Dunlop, the first Collector, took possession of Ahmedabad on 30 November 1817, the city was a sad sight. The walls were broken down in places. Deserted buildings were filled with debris and vegetable growth. People were unwilling to spend any more on the repair of their houses than was needed to prevent them falling down. Wild animals and even wilder Bhils and Kolis, mounted or on foot, roamed within the walls at night or even in the daytime. Bands of them rested in the Shahibaug, the gardens made by Shah Jahan just north of the city. The women and dyers of the city were accustomed to hiring armed men to protect them while they washed at the tanks and river. One of Dunlop's first requests was for more police and more muskets to deal with these marauders.

Dunlop wrote of the contrast between the city as it had once been and as it was in 1817:

> During the reigns of the Mahomedan princes of Ahmedabad, the trade of the place (from the accounts provided) appears to have been so great as to be now scarcely credible, and the extent of the city and its suburbs (still distinctly marked by the ruins) must have been about three times as large as the space now enclosed by the walls, but of which latter, even a great portion is in as deserted a condition as that without, tho' some pooras, or suburbs, continue to be inhabited, in consequence of the enormous duties levied on goods entering the city.[10]

[9] Resident Baroda to Bombay, 15 June 1818, Selections (unprinted) Vol. 145, p. 119 (I).

[10] Collector to Bombay, 28 Dec. 1817, R.D. 125/1818 (I). The accounts referred to no longer survive.

In the reign of Aurangzeb in the late seventeenth century, the octroi (duty on the imports and exports of the city) had been two and a half per cent for Muslims and five per cent for Hindus (though it may be doubted whether these precise amounts were collected). But the channels of trade were now choked by extortionate and vexatious dues of every sort, not only those imposed or increased by the Marathas for revenue purposes, but also many which were collected on behalf of charities or individuals with established customary rights. The Nagarseth, for instance, in recognition of his dignity and services to the community, had the right to collect a proportion of the dues levied on goods imported into the city and into the suburb of Madhavpura. Most of the imposts had probably originated with the farmers of customs and local officials rather than with the central government. Total duties on imports and exports into the city were between fifteen and twenty-five per cent, though these enormous nominal duties were far from being realized in practice. There was widespread evasion and merchants would make private arrangements with the tax collectors, threatening to send their goods elsewhere if the established rates were enforced. Still the high duties did restrict trade and industry, and depopulated the city since they raised the cost of living, even necessities of life like grain and firewood being severely taxed. To the duties was added the burden of the insecurities and costs of road transport. In 1818 merchants were being plundered only six or seven miles from Ahmedabad. These charges were added to the losses the merchants suffered from the decline of their princely and aristocratic markets.[11]

At first the British provided little more than an umbrella of good government for Ahmedabad similar to that which had existed under the Mughals, if less colourful. Andrew Dunlop

[11] Collector to Bombay, 11 Apr. 1818, R.D. 130/1818, and 21 Jan. 1818, R.D. 126/1818 (I).

saw that the city's prosperity could be revived, or rather, given
the right conditions, would revive itself. Ahmedabad was fortunate in her first Collector. He combined an optimistic faith in
the recovery of the city with, so his seniors thought, "fos-
tering care and attention to the usages and prejudices of its inhabitants, as well as to their general interests."[12] He realized the
importance, both for the revival of the city and for ease of
government, of respecting the traditional customs of the
people. Like his famous contemporaries Elphinstone and Mun-
ro, he was no mere defender of tradition for its own sake, but
looked forward to a cautious improvement. This tone was
characteristic of his generation of administrators, which succeeded the conservatives of the eighteenth century but preceded the radical reformers of the second quarter of the nineteenth century. It would be too much to attribute Ahmedabad's
progress to her fortune in the British officers she had been
given, as did Mary Carpenter in 1868, but it was still important
that the first Collector was a man who carefully studied the
city placed in his charge and fought for the measures which
would expedite its recovery.[13] Nor was Dunlop thinking entirely of British interests in his concern for the revival of trade.
He was not interested in opening up Ahmedabad as a market
for British textiles, rather he looked to the revival of her own
indigenous handicrafts.

He asked that the duties on imports and exports into the
city be reduced, though they were the main source of government revenue from Ahmedabad. He realized that any attempt
to collect in full at the old nominal rates, which were not
actually paid under the corrupt and careless Maratha administration but were subject to bargaining, would bring about a
stagnation of trade. Such wisdom was not always displayed in
the early British land revenue collections in India. In Bombay,

[12] Bombay to Commissioner, 14 Dec. 1830, R.D. 12/293/1830 (I).
[13] M. Carpenter, I, 42, 63 (III).

the Customs Committee agreed that "great encouragement and protection should be extended to the trade and inhabitants" of Ahmedabad.[14] The government expected that any temporary loss in tax receipts would be balanced by the growth of trade, the drawing of capitalists to Ahmedabad, and the larger market which the recovery of the city would provide for the agricultural classes.[15] Even if it had been financially possible, the government would not have wanted to completely dispense with town duties because, in the absence of an income tax, the merchants and financiers would then have escaped all taxation. However it recognised that until trade recovered, the burden on this class should be as light as possible.[16] From October 1819, the rate of duty was to be two and a half per cent on all imports and exports, except the raw materials of manufacture, which were to be allowed in duty-free. All private rights to collect dues on the trade of the city were to be abolished or commuted for fixed cash allowances from the treasury.

Dunlop later wrote about the reduction in town duties: "The liberality of this conduct produced the most favourable impression on the inhabitants, and excited a spirit of commercial activity, and enterprize, scarcely to be surpassed."[17] The Ahmedabad merchants at once sent word to their principal markets and received large orders for manufactures at the new lower prices. In fact the system did not work in quite the simple way Dunlop had intended. An extra duty called the *naka* was also imposed, graduated to discriminate against small consignments. There was also the wall tax (to be discussed in chapter IV). Most imported goods actually paid about four per cent. On the other hand, many imported

[14] Report of Customs Committee, 24 Jan. 1818, R.D. 126/1818 (I).

[15] Minute of 16 Sept. 1820 on Collector to Bombay, 29 Aug. 1820, R.D. 159/1820 (I).

[16] Elphinstone's report, 6 Apr. 1821, R.D. 3/27/1822 (I).

[17] Commissioner's circuit report, 20 Jul. 1830, R.D. 12/293/1830 (I).

items in no way connected with the manufactures of the city
were exempted from duty.[18] In practice the system was still
complicated and vexatious and manipulated to the advantage
of the influential, though there is also no doubt that it was a
considerable improvement over that which had existed in
Maratha times.

Under the new duties, industry and trade certainly recovered, though not to the extent Dunlop had hoped. Reports
and statistics are available for a few years only, but these show
the trends and some of the short- and long-term factors affecting the trade of the city. After the first year of the reduced
duties Dunlop was able to report that the value of imports and
exports for the year 1819–20 was 5,469,440 rupees, as against
3,018,169 for the previous year. Although half the increase was
accounted for by the high price of grain due to scarcity, there
had also been several misfortunes: a failure of the cotton crop,
a shortage of raw silk, and a cholera epidemic. The receipts
from duties had fallen from 345,553 to 165,953 rupees, including a loss of 25,000 rupees because of a temporary exemption
of grain from duty. The government was duly gratified by the
increase in trade. But in the next few years the trade did not
increase further, and this was attributed by the then Collector,
Mr. Crawford, to the speculation in *ant* (see below), which
made business hazardous because of fluctuating rates, to the
decline in demand for kinkhab from the Deccan after the annexation of the Peshwa's dominions, and to the government's
prohibition in 1820 of trade with Mocha and other ports in the
Persian Gulf belonging to the Imam of Senna. These ports
formerly took five to six hundred thousand rupees worth of fine
textiles a year.[19] In 1830 Andrew Dunlop, now Revenue Com-

[18] Collector to Bombay, 25 Oct. 1819, J.D. 115/1819; Report on town
duties by J. Langford, R.D. 106/1069/1839 (I).
[19] Collector to Bombay, 29 Aug. 1820, R.D. 159/1820; 22 Aug. 1825,
R.D. 5/137/1826; and 20 Sept. 1825, R.D. 7/117/1825 (I).

missioner, noted in his circuit report that much of the commercial enterprise of Ahmedabad had gone into the opium
trade, but concluded that the regular trade of Ahmedabad had
still increased surprisingly and the city continued to thrive.[20]
In 1839 Ahmedabad was "in a most flourishing condition and
progressing rapidly."[21]

As before, Ahmedabad's main exports were silk and cotton
cloth and brocades; the imports included foodstuffs and raw
silk and cotton. There were also new commodities for the
"Europe shops" opened by Parsis. Among these were English
cotton thread and cloth, first sold in Ahmedabad by Dr. Gilder
and henceforth known as *doctori kapda* (doctor's cloth). Ahmedabad was being subjected to the competition which had
ruined Dacca. Yet the Ahmedabad textile industry survived as
the most important in the city. In 1900, there were estimated to
be ten thousand weavers in the city and in 1914, one thousand
hand looms were still in use.[22]

Ahmedabad's experience was different from Dacca's
largely because the nature of her textile production was different. Dacca's staple, fine muslin, was especially vulnerable
to the competition of English power-looms which could produce cloth of high count more cheaply than the hand loom
weavers, and undersell the Indian product in world markets
and even in India itself. On the other hand, the staples of

Year	Imports	Exports	Total trade
1819–20	(Rupees) 3,870,328	1,599,112	5,469,440
1820–1	3,135,250	1,540,983	4,676,233
1821–2	3,855,638	1,543,238	5,398,876
1822–3	3,250,581	1,609,654	4,860,235
1823–4	3,069,757	1,613,053	4,682,810

R.D. 5/137/1826 (I).

[20] R.D. 12/293/1830 (I).
[21] R.D. 133/1217/1840, p. 155 (minute) (I).
[22] Revenue Dept. (Famine) Res. 2977, 31 July, 1900 (I); A. B. Trivedi, p. 104 (III).

Ahmedabad were not muslins, but coarse dyed cotton cloth, and more important, printed cottons, silks, and brocades, which were less vulnerable to English competition. There was some competition from the Lancashire mills, but not to the extent that ruined Dacca and was once wrongly assumed to have destroyed the competitive position of all Indian cotton textiles. This was not true of Ahmedabad nor of the rural areas of Gujarat. It was noted in 1849 that while the importation of English cloth had almost entirely superseded the weaving of fine cotton cloth in the Ahmedabad district, the coarse variety could still compete because of its cheapness and strength.[23] In 1872, the Bombay Government reported that most of the lower classes in the Bombay Presidency still wore homespun and hand woven cloth.[24] The hand loom weavers of coarse cotton cloth in Gujarat did not succumb to British competition, but to that of India's own textile mills, a much later development. Of Kaira District it was noted in the Gazetteer in 1879: "Until the opening of steam factories at Ahmedabad and Nadiad (1870–1876) the spinning and weaving of cotton cloth was, next to agriculture, the most important industry of the district . . . . the wearing cloth, which, from its greater strength and cheapness had little to fear from the competition of European piece goods, has now been to a great extent ousted by the produce of Bombay and Gujarat weaving mills."[25] And in 1890 one visitor said of Ahmedabad: "In spite of the rapid growth of cotton mills in India, the hand-weaving of cotton cloth still thrives in the city," though the same writer believed the hand loom industry was doomed.[26] English thread, now used by the Indian hand loom

[23] Fawcett, p. 70 (II).
[24] Bombay Government, *General Report on the Administration* 1872–3, p. 367 (II).
[25] *Gazetteer, Kaira and Panch Mahals*, p. 75 (II).
[26] Caine, p. 63 (III).

weavers, was a greater threat to its indigenous counterpart, although many poor people were still employed in spinning country thread throughout the nineteenth century.

Nor did Ahmedabad quickly lose its market for fine fabrics, though prices and returns to the weavers were lower than in the days when there were many more grandees in India. The silks of Ahmedabad were largely immune to foreign competition until well into the second half of the century. Her kinkhab was still celebrated and sought after by the wealthy from all parts of India, and found new markets in Thailand and China. There were still many Indian courts, many of them in Gujarat itself, especially in Saurashtra, which were barely touched by British social influence until well into the second half of the nineteenth century. Except for its Parsi community, the same was true of Gujarat as a whole. While others were welcome to take to the English dress and adopt the English culture, almost as their own, Gujarat produced Mahatma Gandhi, and Ranchhodlal Chhotalal, the pioneer of Ahmedabad's modern textile industry and champion of many modern improvements in the city, who chose to stay away from a reception to a visiting Governor of Bombay because official etiquette required that a "native gentleman" wear English-style shoes or none at all, and he, accustomed to his Gujarati shoes, thought that he would be laughed at in the streets in English shoes. The Hindus, Jains, and Muslims of Gujarat never aped the English or hurried to buy their products in preference to their own.

All the same, it is true that the traders of the city did benefit in new ways. There was the trade in European articles, such as cloth, wines and spirits, and guns and ammunition for hunting, in the "Europe shops" of the Parsis, for instance. Many also benefited as middlemen through the increase of cotton production for export, particularly from Ahmedabad and Broach districts. Ahmedabadis established cotton gins and presses in villages and small towns and advanced money to the farmers. Others, especially Parsis, became rich as contractors for the British, supplying grain and other commodities to their cantonments and lending money to their soldiers and officers.

Opium was another source of wealth for the Vanias of Ahmedabad, and it was an immensely lucrative one. This trade expanded greatly soon after the beginning of British rule because the East India Company needed to find something, other than specie, which the Chinese would accept in exchange for their silk and tea. The opium was grown in Malwa, where it was bought by merchants, many of them from Ahmedabad, and carried on pack animals to the ports. Until 1831 the East India Company had a legal monopoly of the purchase of Malwa opium, but this did not stop the development of a considerable illegal traffic, which continued after the government substituted an export duty. Much of the opium passed through non-British territory to Karachi or Daman and from there was sent to East Asia. The profits were very large. In Ahmedabad the business of trading in opium with China started in 1819 and much capital and many people soon became involved. By 1830 almost all the Ahmedabad merchants had agents or branches of their houses established in Malwa for the purchase of opium.[27] In 1849 a British officer estimated that upwards of 5,000,000 rupees capital was employed in the opium trade in Ahmedabad, as against only 500,000 to 600,000 rupees in the export trade in cotton.[28] Insurance was effected regularly and cheaply at Ahmedabad in the traditional manner. Most of the opium was sold to other merchants, including those in Bombay, but some of the Ahmedabad merchants traded with China on their own account. Several large fortunes were amassed; it is said

[27] Commissioner's circuit report, 20 Jul. 1830, R.D. 12/293/1830 (I).
[28] Fawcett, pp. 82–88 (II).

that in one particularly good year the profit to Ahmedabad's merchants reached 10,000,000 rupees.[29] However, the trade was uncertain and dependent on such outside variables as the actions of the Chinese Government and East India Company in China and the British occupation of Sind in 1843, which stopped the illegal export trade through Karachi. Several fortunes were lost. Some of the most respectable financiers of Ahmedabad did not engage in the trade because of the risks involved, and as a result some of them lost their pre-eminence in Ahmedabad to others who were more enterprising.[30]

Another source of wealth for some, and of loss for others, was gambling by means of anticipation bargains (*vaida*) on the rise and fall of opium prices in Calcutta or cotton prices in Bombay or sugar prices. Contracts would be made to deliver so much of a commodity at a stated price on a specified day in the future, on the understanding that on that day only the cash difference between the stated price and the market price on that day would change hands. Even children speculated with small amounts in this way.[31] The share mania that gripped Western India at the time of the rise in cotton prices during the American Civil War, which made and then unmade many fortunes (though more in Bombay than in Ahmedabad), was a symptom of an ever-present tendency in the Indian business classes. It is said that during one session of the Indian National Congress at Ahmedabad the speech of the chairman of the reception committee was interrupted by shouted quotations and bids across the floor.

In addition to this speculation on commodity prices, there was also speculation in ant. This was a unique fictitious currency invented in Ahmedabad during the disorders of the eighteenth century, when it was risky to transfer bullion and the coinage was being depreciated. A transaction in ant was

[29] *Ahmedabad Gazetteer*, p. 64 (II).
[30] Maganlal Vakhatchand, p. 146 (III).
[31] *Ahmedabad Gazetteer*, pp. 66–67 (II).

ment's intention in counting them.[36] As early as 1820 Andrew
Dunlop reported that there was extensive immigration into
Ahmedabad district from the neighbouring districts of the
Gaikwad's dominions, showing the improved conditions
under British rule. The immigrants in 1826—mostly Kanbis
and Neerada Rajputs—cited cruel and oppressive treatment
by the Gaikwad's officers as their reason for emigrating. Many
merchants and artisans were returning to Ahmedabad.[37] "Once
more the weavers almost in a body deserted Pattan."[38]
But some of the military class, not finding encouragement and
employment under the British, were leaving.

In 1872 there were in Ahmedabad 92,619 Hindus and
Jains (11,763 of the latter), 23,491 Muslims (including 1,594
Bohoras), 446 Parsis, 40 Jews, and 264 Christians. This undoubtedly represented a different composition from that
which had existed in Muslim and Maratha days, though there
are no reliable figures for those days. At the 1824 survey,
there had been 22,282 Hindu, 6,913 Muslim, and 4 Parsi
houses in the city. It is probable that the proportion of Muslims had fallen faster in the late eighteenth century, since
many of the official and military class, and their retainers,
left the city to her Maratha rulers. The decline of the Muslim families of high status continued under the British. There
were no longer the openings for Muslim courtiers, officials,
scholars, and soldiers that Muslim rule had provided. Many
of these people left the city. The percentage of Hindus and
Jains in the population of the city rose from 76.31 in 1824 to
79.24 in 1872. Of the Khadia division, it was written in 1879:
"The Musulmans, numbering a little more than one-sixth of
the whole population, are chiefly Bohoras of both sects. Of

[36] Maganlal Vakhatchand, p. 131 (III).
[37] Collector's report 1820, R.D. 17/1821; Collector to Bombay, 27
Sept. 1826, R.D. 19/151/1826; and 29 Aug. 1820, R.D. 159/1820 (I).
[38] *Baroda Gazetteer*, p. 156 (II).

other Musulmans there are not many, and their general poverty is driving them into the poorer quarters of the city,
while their houses pass into the hands of the thrifty Jain and
other Vanias."[39]

The Parsis and Jews followed the British to the city and
the Christians were new converts, but these communities
have held a minor place in Ahmedabad. By 1843 there were
enough Parsis in the city for a tower of silence to be built,
and in 1846 a fire-temple. An Ahmedabad Parsi Panchayat
was founded by Mancherji Sorabji Karanjawala, a merchant
whose son Kavasji later became important in municipal politics in Ahmedabad. One of the first Parsi residents of Ahmedabad was Pestonji Framji Vakil, whose son Nowroji
Pestonji Vakil was one of the leading seths of Ahmedabad
in the later nineteenth century, an important contractor for
building roads, railways, storehouses, and a salt agent, opium
agent, and *abkari* (liquor tax) contractor. A Roman Catholic
chapel was built in 1842 and the English Church in 1848, and
the Irish Presbyterian Church began missionary work in the
city and surrounding country in 1861. The Christian missionaries made few converts in Ahmedabad and their social
influence was not great except for their work in education.

On the whole, wealth and social eminence remained for
the time being in the possession of the established trading
and financial families. These bought and sold the cotton,
opium, and textiles and financed the trade and industry which
brought wealth to the city. One of the largest firms was that
of the Nagarseth family, the firm of Vakhatchand Khushal-
chand. This played an important part in the revenue administration of various Gujarat states. Hemabhai Vakhatchand
was a leading participant in the opium trade. His son,
Premabhai was described as a millionaire, though he lost

[39] *Ahmedabad Gazetteer*, pp. 293, 317, and 323 (II).

money during the share mania of 1864–65.[40] A son-in-law
who became immensely rich through the opium trade was
Hathising Kesrising, whose father had been a dealer in raw
silk. Hathising's wealth was said to have amounted to 8,000,-
000 rupees at his death in 1845. He spent 1,000,000 rupees on
the construction of a Jain temple, completed in 1848 and a
landmark in Ahmedabad today; if not of great architectural
distinction, it is nonetheless impressive.[41]

By the mid-nineteenth century, there had been a loosening
of the tight social bonds of the old city, an expansiveness, a
return of the confidence of earlier days. In 1849 a British
officer remarked about the wealthy people of the city:

> The condition of the people is, I am informed by respectable
> inhabitants, much improved since the late Mahratta Govern-
> ment. In those times a wealthy man was not known by his
> dress, carriage, or appearance; and if a person attempted to
> show his wealth, he was very soon under some pretext or
> other deprived of it. The habits which this produced are now
> wearing off, and the wealthy of the city have many of them
> set up carriages, and several have built country houses, and
> enjoy themselves in the ease and comfort which characterizes
> a peaceful and civilized people. The native Hindu population
> are undoubtedly in better circumstances than the Mahome-
> dans. There are a few wealthy Mussulmans, who trade in silk
> and piece goods, but the majority of Mussulmans seek for
> employment as peons or weavers or as labourers.[42]

In 1851 Maganlal Vakhatchand referred to the building of
houses in the English style, with many glass windows, and to
some changes in dress, including the wearing of socks.[43] One
of the first to leave the pols to live in a bungalow was Hathis-

[40] Malabari, pp. 108–109 (III).
[41] Edalji Dosabhai, p. 283 (III).
[42] Fawcett, p. 70 (II).
[43] Maganlal Vakhatchand, pp. 140, 128 (III).

ing Kesrising, who built a large house in a neoclassical style, with Western furniture and Chinese curios, near his Jain temple, outside the Delhi gate on the way to Shahibaug. Other prominent seths built bungalows also.

The British presence was never obtrusive in Ahmedabad, as it was in Calcutta or the other cities they had built up as their own, or had made into military stations like Poona. Ahmedabad never had a sizeable English business community, as did other cities of its size and commercial and industrial importance. The Ahmedabadis kept them out. The British held their reins on Ahmedabad lightly. Indeed they could do little else at the beginning and for many years after. There were never very many English civilians or soldiers in Ahmedabad. The station did not enjoy a good reputation: it was unhealthy, there were few amusements or amenities for Europeans, and the dust and climate were trying, especially the furnace of May and June. The British cantonment, the headquarters of the northern division of the Bombay Army, was 3½ miles north of the walled city. The English civil officers at Ahmedabad included the Collector (District Magistrate), the District Judge, the Executive Engineer, the Civil Surgeon, the Superintendent and Assistant Superintendent of Police, and the City Survey Officer. The bulk of the administration and police was, of course, Indian. When the British took over, their own officers were substituted for the Maratha ones at the top, the few non-hereditary officials were discharged, but the holders of hereditary posts, by far the more numerous, were confirmed in them. Religious and charitable pensions and allowances were continued, as were pensions awarded for past services to the Mughal and Maratha Governments: where the allowance was hereditary, it was continued under the British; where it was non-hereditary it remained so under the British and lapsed on the death of the recipient. The East India Company acted as the legal successor of those governments. Incidentally, the old Muslim and Maratha *sanads* (deeds of grant) produced before the British officials, and preserved in copy in the files of the Bombay Government, show a respect for learning and holiness wherever it was to be found, among Hindus and Muslims alike. The British cannot be reproached on this score either, though there were the inevitable complaints by aggrieved individuals whose claims could not be substantiated by the production of documents or were successfully disputed by relatives.[44]

The British also paid respect to the traditional offices of the City. The Kazi, described as "respectable and learned," retained his office and, although supplanted in many of his judicial functions by the British courts, was appointed Muhammadan Law Officer to the Court of Adalat (that is, adviser in cases of Muslim law), a post he held for 22 years, to be succeeded by his son. His brother was made Faujdar of the City and served for 27 years.[45] The Kazi registered marriages and deaths among the Muslims and was also called upon to settle disputes within the Muslim community. In general the Ahmedabadis are not given to litigation and prefer to settle disputes privately rather than in the courts. The Kazi was regarded by the British officers as the head of the Muslim community and was consulted on matters affecting it. The post remains hereditary in the same family to this day. The same is true of the Padshahi Diwan family; an allowance was granted to this former Mughal functionary though he was no longer required to perform any official services. Similarly,

[44] R.D. 24/884/1838, p. 38; Collector to Bombay, 19 Jan. 1819, R.D. 137/1819 (I). In 1819, the number of official pensions, charitable allowances, and grants to Hindu temples and Muslim shrines in Ahmedabad City was 355, at a total cost to the government of 16,993 rupees.

[45] J.D. 102/1818; Petition of Mahomed Hoosein Oodean, R.D. 196/1845 (I).

the Nagarseth was given deference as the most important
Hindu and Jain personage of the city, was looked upon as
the head of the sarafs of the city, and was the medium of
communication between them and the government on particular occasions. He was allowed to continue to collect certain hereditary dues on goods passing through Madhavpura,
but was granted an annual allowance in lieu of his rights to
collect dues on the imports and exports of the city proper.
The Nagarseth and the Kazi were appointed as a matter of
course to all committees of importance set up in the city by
the government or by the people, and petitions from the people of the city to the government were signed by them.

The influence of the sarafs and their customary power over
the affairs of the city and its administration is illustrated by a
curious incident which occurred a few years after the British
administration began. An embezzlement of 47,000 rupees
from the Collector's treasury was found; it had taken place
some time between 1818 and 1824, but it was never dis-
covered how and the money was never recovered. During
the investigations, the Collector was astonished to find that
the sarafs had long been accustomed to using the public treasury as a bank (and a rather accommodating one at that),
depositing cash or drawing warrants on district treasuries for
hundreds of thousands of rupees without paying in an equivalent amount in cash to the central treasury. The treasurer
kept private accounts with almost all the sarafs of the city. He
was convicted but the eminently respectable sarafs, who included the Nagarseth, could see nothing wrong with their
conduct and were not prosecuted.[46] It is likely that there
were many unrecorded cases where the sarafs and important
mahajans of Ahmedabad were able to influence the subordinate administration to their own advantage, especially in the

[46] R.D. 157/1827, pp. 191–318 (I).

collection of town duties. Incidentally, it was also the practice in Jaipur State, which in the eighteenth century was known as the "Bania Raj," for sahukars to use the treasury's funds, which freely circulated in the market.[47] The sarafs and merchants of Ahmedabad traditionally enjoyed a reputation for honesty; transactions involving enormous amounts of money were once carried on in Gujarat verbally, and a legendary saraf was advanced a large sum on the security of a hair of his moustache. Standards of commercial morality have declined in modern times, possibly as a result of the greater social mobility and opportunities afforded by British rule accompanied by the substitution of codified law for custom.[48] As the power of the richer sarafs waned, so did their control over standards.

In the nineteenth century, the dominance of the old, established firms was reduced, the middle of the social pyramid was broadened, and the financial predominance of the Jains was impaired by the Vaishnava Vanias, the Patidars, and some Parsis. An early incident illustrates the weakening of the old elite. In 1827 the Jain Vanias petitioned the Governor of Bombay to compel the Vaishnavas to continue to pay an old levy on exports for the maintenance of the panjarapol.[49] They had heard that the Vaishnavas intended in future to divert the funds to their *maharaj*. The Vaishnava mahajans, on their part, petitioned the government to order the continued collection of levies for their charities—the feeding of the poor, the maintenance of rest-houses for travellers, and the support of holy men. They asked that the Jains and Muslims be made to pay as be-

---

[47] Bhargava, p. 233 (III).
[48] Malabari, pp. 111–112 (III).
[49] On a typical day in 1875 this animal home housed 265 cows and bullocks, 130 buffaloes, 5 blind cattle, 894 goats, 20 horses, 7 cats, 2 monkeys, 274 fowls, 290 ducks, 2000 pigeons, 50 parrots, 25 sparrows, 5 kites, 33 miscellaneous birds, and an uncountable number of insects in a special room (*Ahmedabad Gazetteer*, p. 115) (II).

fore. In both cases the government declined to interfere, noting that the former governments had not actually enforced the payment of these levies, although they had probably strongly recommended it. In 1839 they were still being collected on a voluntary basis but the response was poor; and by 1879 it was the practice for the money collected from Jains to go to their animal homes, from the Vaishnavas to their temples, from the Khojas to the Aga Khan, and from the other Muslims to local shrines.[50]

The mahajans were now less able to enforce penalties against individuals, who were given the protection of the courts. In 1896 Hopkins observed that although the guilds were still vigorous in Ahmedabad, their power was rapidly declining. They tended to admit outsiders more readily and to become more formal in their organization. There were now constitutions and elected officers and more internal democracy, with less control by the hereditary seths and patels. The latter was true of castes too. There were caste reform associations which made such changes as the replacement of wasteful expenditure on caste dinners and ceremonial occasions by charities and scholarships. This type of caste reform association was more important in nineteenth century Ahmedabad than non-caste, voluntary associations of the modern kind. There was also a tendency for the caste to lose some of its restrictive and coercive aspects and to become more of an agency for mutual help. By 1911 there had been a weakening of the control of caste *panchayats* over such matters as the performance of marriage promises or betrothals, questions of maintenance, and runaway wives. The authority of the Vaishnava *maharajas* was also in decline.[51] The trades in opium, raw cotton, and European

[50] Petitions, 9 Jul. 1827, G.D. 13/146/1827; and 8 Oct. 1827, G.D. 170/1828; Report on town duties by J. Langford, R.D. 106/1069/1839 (I); *Ahmedabad Gazetteer*, p. 112 (II).

[51] Hopkins, pp. 199, 204, 186 (III); *Ahmedabad Gazetteer*, pp. 107–112; *Census of India 1911*, Vol. VII, pp. 199–201 (II).

goods and the contracts with the British as provisioners gave opportunities to ambitious individuals, but in the nineteenth century, it was only a rare person who was creative outside the boundaries of his caste tradition. There is no evidence that there was any loosening of the family structure in the nineteenth century, and the other changes mentioned above were very limited. Neera Desai has written: "A new direction to social change was imparted to the Gujarati society during the nineteenth century and it experienced a qualitative transformation (however limited it may be) which lifted it to a new type of social structure founded on the basis of achievement, secularism, and legal-rational norms."[52] Here the qualification "limited" should be emphasized. It was not until the twentieth century, when the walls came down and the women came out and the Patidar immigrants rose to their present eminence, that Ahmedabad really opened out.

The progress of Western higher education was slow in Ahmedabad, slower than in neighbouring Maharashtra, which was also part of the Bombay Presidency. The first two government vernacular schools were opened in 1826, but the first government English school not until 1846. The decade after 1856 saw more progress. In 1878 there were 23 government schools with an average total attendance of 2049 pupils, including one high school and two training colleges. There were also six private schools with an average total attendance of 545 pupils. In 1856, on the initiative of the Collector, Mr. T. C. Hope, the community raised 50,000 rupees to start a college to prepare youths for government employment. In 1861 a law lectureship was established with these funds and classes in general education were added later; in 1873 the classes were discontinued because of poor results. But in 1879 an arts college was opened after public interest had been displayed and further

[52] Desai, "Gujarati Society in Nineteenth Century," p. 536 (III).

subscriptions raised, and students from Ahmedabad were also beginning to go to Bombay for higher studies.[53] But Ahmedabad's response to higher education so far had indicated no remarkable interest in acquiring Western learning, nor, except for the Nagar Brahmin caste with its tradition of government service, in gaining admission to the government service or the legal profession. In 1885 there were only six graduates in Ahmedabad, eighteen pleaders, and three licentiates of medicine, surgery, and civil engineering.[54]

A more important influence than attendance at Western schools was provided by contact with British officers, and this influence can be seen working in the Gujarat Vernacular Society, in the social reform movement, and in the activities of Ranchhodlal Chhotalal, the father of modern Ahmedabad, whose achievements will take up much of the next two chapters.

The Gujarat Vernacular Society, which became an important medium for propagating the ideas of those who wished to consciously change Gujarat society, was founded in 1848 by Alexander Kinloch Forbes, a scholarly English officer who had been appointed Assistant Judge at Ahmedabad two years earlier. Its objects were the encouragement of vernacular literature and education and the collection of printed books and manuscripts. In Forbes's words, he aimed "to lift up the language of the province from its present ignoble condition."[55] Like many other Indian languages, Gujarati was then very undeveloped, and its progress into a refined, literary language owes much to the Gujarat Vernacular Society and its press. At first all the members of the Managing Committee were Englishmen but Indians were added later. The first

---

[53] Education Commission, *Evidence* (Mahipatram's testimony), 1884, II, 446; *Ahmedabad Gazetteer*, 309 (II).
[54] Appendix to Municipal *Report* 1896–97 (II).
[55] Parekh, *Gujarat Vernacular Society no Itihasa* Vol. I, p. 10 (III).

newspaper in Gujarat, a weekly called *Vartman*, was started
by the Society in 1849 and the first public library in the same
year. In 1857, after Nagarseth Hemabhai Vakhatchand donated the money for a new hall, the library was renamed the
Hemabhai Institute. In 1850 the Society took over a co-
educational school which had been opened by Karunashanker
Dayashanker and a girls' school begun by the widow of
Hathising Kesrising. In 1851 its press began to print books for
use in the vernacular schools, a Gujarati grammar, and other
works. In 1854 the Society took over a monthly called *Buddhi
Prakash*. Translations into Gujarati were encouraged and there
were prizes for Gujarati writing, including one to Maganlal
Vakhatchand for his history of Ahmedabad.[56] As might be
expected from this city, essay competitions were set on such
eminently practical subjects as banks, encouragement to indigenous crafts, local self-government, famines, as well as on
social reform topics.[57] Most of the prominent leaders of Ahmedabad who figure in this book in other contexts were Presidents of the Gujarat Vernacular Society at one time.

The pioneer of the religious reform which can definitely
be ascribed to Western influence was Bholanath Sarabhai, a
Vadnagara Nagar Brahmin and a first-class subordinate judge
in the British service. Bholanath's conversion to religious reform followed his reading of Dr. Blair's sermons, a book recommended to him by Ranchhodlal Chhotalal. He discarded
idolatry and became in the end a pure theist. In 1858 he organised a Dharma Samaj which met weekly for religious
discourses and published collections of religious poems. In
1871 Bholanath and others founded the Prarthana Samaj at
Ahmedabad. Its leading lights were Bholanath Sarabhai, Mahipatram Rupram, and Lalshankar Umiashankar. The Prar-

[56] *Reports of Gujarat Vernacular Society, 1849, 1854–5* (III); *Ahmedabad Gazetteer*, pp. 310–311 (II).
[57] Desai, "Gujarati Society in Nineteenth Century," p. 338 (III).

thana Samaj bodies of Bombay, Ahmedabad, and other cities of
western India were the counterparts of the Brahmo Samaj of
Bengal. They had congregational worship, were monotheistic,
and were generally similar in doctrine and aims. On the question of the origin of the Ahmedabad Prarthana Samaj, Bholanath's son and biographer concludes: "How far Bholanath's
original idea was influenced and informed by the Brahmo
movement, it is difficult to ascertain. But even if it had any
influence it was more of a propelling than an informing power.
. . . there is no doubt whatever that Bholanath had conceived
the idea of some sort of religious movement long before he ever
heard of the Brahmo Samaj of Calcutta."[58] It is impossible to
say whether this view is correct, or whether Bholanath was
influenced by developments in Bombay, where he attended a
theist prayer meeting in 1869. It is significant perhaps that at
about that time, Satyendranath Tagore, of the famous Bengali
family and a Brahmo, was Assistant Judge in Ahmedabad. He
gave lectures to the Prarthana Samaj and together with Bholanath translated Bengali prayers into Gujarati. Devendranath
Tagore and Pratapa Chandra Mazumdar visited Ahmedabad,
and Bholanath visited Calcutta. Swami Dayananda, the founder
of the Arya Samaj, came to Ahmedabad and tried to persuade
Bholanath to change the name of his society to "Arya Samaj,"
but Bholanath was not prepared to accept Dayananda's doctrine of the infallibility and sole authority of the *vedas*. Dayananda then tried to found an Arya Samaj at Ahmedabad but this
did not take root.

By the late nineteenth century it was apparent that the
Prarthana Samaj would remain a small body with only marginal
influence on the main body of Hindu opinion and practice in
Gujarat. As one conservative critic wrote: "It completed the
alienation of the Reform party from the main body of the

[58] Krishnarao Bholanath, p. 6 (III).

people. Subservient to the spirit of active hostility to the existing modes and institutions of religious worship, it sounded the
death knell of the reform cause."[59]

Closely connected with religious reform was the cause of
social reform: by this is meant here the problems of widow
remarriage, child marriage, the education of women, and caste
restrictions, including those on foreign travel. These matters
became important subjects of public debate in Ahmedabad, just
as they did elsewhere in India. The leading figures in the social
reform movement were Bholanath Sarabhai and Mahipatram
Rupram Nilkanth. Both were Vadnagara Nagar Brahmins, a
caste which produced many notable scholars and able administrators under the Mughals, Marathas, and British. Both were
government servants. Mahipatram was an officer in the Education Department who became Principal of the Gujarat Training College in 1861 after having been sent to England in 1860
to study teachers' training colleges there. For many years
afterwards he was a cause célèbre because of his breach of caste
rules in crossing the waters. The reformers started societies in
Ahmedabad to campaign against child marriage (the Gujarat
Hindu Social Reform Association) and against the prohibition
of the remarriage of widows. Most of the prominent seths and
millowners of nineteenth century Ahmedabad contributed in
some way to social reform, through the endowment of girls'
schools or in working for a liberalization of their caste rules and
the substitution of more worthy charities for the extravagant
caste dinners. But some of them were lukewarm in their support, and others, like Ranchhodlal Chhotalal, were much more
cautious in their approach than Bholanath or Mahipatram.

How deep was the influence of the reformers? Mary Carpenter, the English reformer, who visited India in 1866 and
1868, was much impressed by what she saw in Ahmedabad.

[59] U.K. Trivedi, p. 844 (III).

She wrote that the influence of a succession of devoted and cultured British officers was reflected in "the advanced tone of the more educated native inhabitants, in the enlightened development of many of the institutions, and in the improvements which are continually going on in the city and its neighbourhood." She went so far as to say: "How remarkable a step had been quietly taken I did not fully appreciate until I had been in Calcutta and other parts of the empire; then I found how very far behind Ahmedabad these other places were, in effort to promote female education among the leading Hindoos,—in emancipation of the ladies from the thraldom imposed by custom,—and in self-effort for improvement on their own part."[60]

In spite of this eulogy, it appears that the influence of the social reformers was largely limited to the spread of education for women, though the results here were impressive. The first girls' schools were started by the Ahmedabadis themselves in the 1850's, well before most other parts of India. Funds were given by the Jain financier, millowner, and philanthropist, Maganbhai Karamchand, and by the widow of Hathising Kesrising; later, the millowner Bechardas Ambaidas endowed the Mahalaksmi Female Training College. The first female university graduates (Vidyagauri and Shardagauri, 1901) had to face public criticism, but there was little opposition in Ahmedabad to the idea of primary or secondary education for girls. Here the leading citizens of Ahmedabad were well in advance of government policy.[61] It was the lack of cultural resistance on this issue in Ahmedabad and north Gujarat—pos-

[60] M. Carpenter, I, 42, 53 (III).

[61] The Government of India resolution of 1868 urged great caution in view of the political and social implications, insisted that the initiative come from the Indians themselves before government aid could be extended, and, quite unmindful of the progress made in Ahmedabad, noted that a demand had been felt only in the three Presidency capitals (*Proceedings* of the Home Department (Education), no. 251:61, 30 Apr. 1868) (I).

sibly stemming in part from the place accorded women in the
Jain religion—rather than the influence of the European officers
or their wives, or any general acceptance of Western ways or
"progressive spirit," which accounts for Mary Carpenter's
good impression. She found the people she talked to "deeply
interested" in the subject of female education. At the home of
Nagarseth Premabhai Hemabhai, she met twenty or thirty
ladies who expressed a desire for the education of their daugh-
ters. She thought this a remarkable gathering. And at Satyendranath Tagore's, where she stayed, she sat at table with Hindu
ladies and gentlemen together, her only such experience in
India. Mary Carpenter's second visit to India was made after
she received a letter from Judge Gopal Row Huri Deshmukh
of Ahmedabad. The city had shown great interest in the cause
of female education, but there were no Indian women teachers
available. During her visit, the Government of India did de-
cide to give funds for the establishment of female normal
schools in the three Presidency capitals, but not in Ahmedabad,
which had shown greater interest than the three capitals.[62]
While she was in Ahmedabad, a public meeting was held to
advocate the remarriage of widows, and in this matter too the
reformers made some progress.

Mary Carpenter found the people she talked to quite un-
concerned about the low caste people in the city, for whom
nothing was being done "to do them good or elevate their
condition." In reply to her enquiry about the education of the
lower castes, one Ahmedabad gentleman replied: "We have
enough to do at present with the education of our own class,
without thinking of these."[63] They seldom sought admission into the schools, and when they did, the higher caste pupils would
tend to leave, and either the schools had to be closed or some

[62] J. E. Carpenter, pp. 361–362 (III).
[63] M. Carpenter, I, 47 (III).

compromise effected. In the second half of the century, separate schools were provided for the lower castes and the
prejudice against their attending the regular schools was
gradually reduced.[64] In this the Missions were pioneers. But
inter-caste marriage and any significant improvement in the
social and economic position of the low caste people had to
wait, first for Mahatma Gandhi, and then for the accelerated
modernization of the mid-twentieth century.

As late as 1850 Ahmedabad looked and indeed was still a
medieval city. Its old institutions were flourishing; the sarafs
and mahajans still dominated trade and industry; the ancient
crafts were still the basis of its prosperity; and its imports and
exports moved on pack animals along the narrow unpaved
lanes, flanked by high, unpainted wooden houses, and through
the guarded gates in its walls. But Ahmedabad could not remain a medieval city for ever. So far it had been lucky in being
in a relatively inaccessible area, and in still having a market
for its products. The twenty years after 1850 saw the breakdown of its isolation and more inroads into its market.

The railway, the bearer of Western industrial civilization
into distant continents in the Victorian age, reached Ahmedabad from Bombay in 1864 and pushed on further north and
west. Ahmedabad became even more important as the largest
trade centre in Gujarat, and this helped to cushion the effects
of the slump in cotton prices and the foolish speculation which
had preceded it. The sea trade through Dholera fell off and
so did the market of Dholka. Ahmedabad became a major
entrepôt for the distribution of imported goods. It was the
junction with the metre-gauge Rajputana-Malwa railway to
Delhi and with the Ahmedabad-Parantij, Godhra-Rutlam,

[64] By 1897 the Municipality was aiding the education of 75 low-caste
boys (40 of them in a separate school) and of 525 Brahmins, 2389 other
Hindus and Jains, 605 Muslims, 27 Parsis, 3 Jews, and 4 tribal people
(Municipal *Report* 1896–97 (II).

and Ahmedabad-Wadhwan railways. There were important
social consequences also. The railway helped to break down
the isolation of the city from outside influences. Journeys to
Ahmedabad by English officers, Bombay businessmen, and
missionaries were faster and more frequent, and so were the
trips of Ahmedabadis to Bombay for business or study—never
for pleasure. Shipments of goods took less time and organization, needed less capital tied up for long periods, and did not
need to be insured. Thus the predominance of the larger Ahmedabad houses was weakened to the advantage of enterprising
clerks and other newcomers. Nor could large profits be gained
now from scarcities in commodities.[65] Finally, the railway
brought the threat of competition from the mills of Bombay
and ensured that Ahmedabad's old reliance on handicraft textile production would have to go.

Early in the second half of the century, there were other
signs that Ahmedabad could not continue indefinitely in the
old way. The traffic in opium was no longer as lucrative as it
had once been; there was competition from domestic Chinese
producers and from other Indian merchants. By 1878 the
opium trade had passed from Ahmedabad to merchants in
Baroda State, and in that year the purchase, manufacture, and
sale of opium in Baroda State became a state monopoly.[66] Also,
the sarafs had lost much of their business as state bankers,
money-lenders to the rulers, and army paymasters. Earlier in
the century, the East India Company had been glad to use the
sarafs, but now the administration preferred to place business
with the new joint-stock banks instead. Moreover Ahmedabad's weavers, dyers, and other handicraft artisans were now
faced with greater outside competition.

In 1873 a petition to the Governor of Bombay from a large

[65] Rogers, I, 47, 68 (III); *Ahmedabad Gazetteer*, pp. 65, 106 (II).
[66] *Ahmedabad Gazetteer*, p. 64; *Baroda Gazetteer*, pp. 130–131 (II).

body of the inhabitants complained of the "rapid decline and decay of the indigenous industrial arts pursued in this town."[67] Ahmedabad had always been famed for its high-quality paper, but this industry fell into decline after the mid-nineteenth century because of competition from France. Calico printing suffered from the competition of cheap European prints, and silk from the industries of Europe and China. The import of raw silk into Ahmedabad fell from 100 tons in 1874, to 65 tons in 1877, and to 41 tons in 1878. Although this was in part due to a temporary shortage and to high grain prices and a dullness of trade, it also reflected Chinese competition and changes in taste and fashion, as women of the Vania and Brahmin castes were taking to Chinese silks. The prices of local silks and the rates of wages of the artisans fell considerably about this time. The impoverishment of the Muslim families of high status who wore kinkhab in waist-coats and jackets, the deposition in 1875 of the Gaikwad Malharrao, who had annually bought from Ahmedabad silk goods of the value of 500,000 rupees and cotton goods worth 300,000 rupees, and the decreasing use of brocades by the other Gujarat princes and chiefs, all resulted in a decline of demands for Ahmedabad's traditional products in the second half of the century.[68] Western influence was spreading inexorably into Gujarat and Rajasthan. The education of the princes along modern lines and the influence of the British rulers were changing taste and fashion. Kinkhab was now worn by them only in state robes; in 1879 it was noted that although it still found a good market in Central India, the demand from Gujarat had fallen off. Illustrative of the change in fashion is the art gallery of one ex-prince of a state in Gujarat, now open to the public, with its expensive array of European paintings (many of them full-scale copies of old masters, others

[67] Petition, 20 Jan. 1873, *Report (and Evidence) of the Finance Committee 1871–1874, P.P.* 1873, XII, 382 (II).
[68] *Ahmedabad Gazetteer*, pp. 133–139 (II).

portraits of the wives of English officers by third-rate English
artists), and Chinese vases. Ahmedabad was losing its market.
A petition from the silk weavers of Kuturwadda, Tanna, could
just as well have come from Ahmedabad: "A Petambar (a kind
of silk dress used by the higher Hindoos at their meals) was
formerly sold for Rupees 24 during the Maratha reign when
the country abounded in grandees—now a days however it
hardly yields Rupees 14." The Bombay Government thought
that silk manufacture deserved encouragement, and removed
the loom-tax on these weavers in 1840, just as it had on the
cotton weavers in 1838.[69] But the decline of the handicrafts
was something government measures could not prevent. Even
high tariffs, incompatible with the free trade ideas of the time,
could not have protected them against changes in taste and
demand.

Ahmedabad had been given a respite, but now she was
faced with that problem of adaptation which is the central
theme in the history of all the non-European peoples in modern
times. Kavi Dalpatram Dahyabhai (a Shrimali Brahmin) was
the herald of the new age in Ahmedabad. In his topical verse
he praised British rule for its order, justice, and progressive
spirit and urged the people of Gujarat to respond favourably
to the new influences coming from the West. Maganlal Vakhatchand had called British rule "Ram Rajya" (the ideal kingdom) and extolled the rule of law, the zeal for improvement
shown by the British, and the lower taxes and prices under the
Pax Britannica—an attitude typical of a generation which was
still close to the disorder of the eighteenth century.[70] But Dalpatram also recognized the challenge of the West for what it
was and, in a poem known to most educated people in the city,
wrote of the "Invasion of Hunnar Khan" (industry) and his

[69] R.D. 130/1214/1840, pp. 159–163 (I).
[70] Maganlal Vakhatchand, p. 139 (III).

minister, Yantra Khan (machinery). Nor was he the only Gujarati writer to urge the learning of European industrial techniques.[71] At a time when the intelligentsia of Bengal was wrestling with the intellectual issues raised by the challenge of the West, Ahmedabad was about to respond in a very different way.

[71] Dalpatram, II, 26–32; Neera Desai, "Gujarati Society in Nineteenth Century," p. 338 (III).

CHAPTER III

The Mills

It was far from inevitable that a modern textile industry should have developed in the city of Ahmedabad. In some ways it was even an unsuitable place for one. The only fuel at hand to fire the boilers of the mills was wood. By 1895 most of the mills were using imported coal, and coal had later to be brought hundreds of miles from Bengal or Central India. As there was no suitable port nearby, imports of machinery, mill stores, and long-staple cotton had to come 300 miles by rail from Bombay. The climate is very dry and there is a tendency for the thread to break in the machines. The Ahmedabad mills have had to pay particular attention to fuel economy and to humidifying. Ahmedabad district is a cotton-growing tract, but although cotton suitable for the production of coarse yarn and cloth is grown near Ahmedabad, much of the long-staple cotton used in later years had to be brought from much further afield (as indeed was the case in Lancashire, New England, and Japan). As early as 1895 the Ahmedabad millowners were importing Egyptian cotton.[1] Ahmedabad is nearer to the markets of north India than Bombay, but the railway rates were unfavourable to her. The railway companies had tariffs which favoured long-distance traffic to and from the ports, since they naturally charged low rates on routes where they had competition from other railway companies and high rates where they had no competition. "Following the policy of undiluted commercialism, Indian railways, even when State owned and State managed, quote very low rates at the competitive points and recoup their loss by raising their rates from the non-competitive centres, to the clear detriment of the national industries."[2] Imported goods had to be sent to Ahmedabad through Bombay on the Bombay, Baroda, and Central India Railway; but those to places in northern and central India could go through Calcutta or in the case of north India, Karachi, as an alternative. On the question of whether the Ahmedabad mills did enjoy any locational advantage over those of Bombay which might account for their greater profitability, one English expert on the textile industry concluded in 1930 that "the so-called geographical advantage can only be very small, if indeed there is any in favour of Ahmedabad."[3] By that time Ahmedabad was using more foreign cotton than Bombay, and was exporting its fine cloth to far-off Calcutta.

To those who believe Western influence and example was decisive in Indian industrialization, Ahmedabad must seem a strange case. It lacked the advantages of centres like Bombay and Calcutta. "Even before independence, Ahmedabad was

[1] *Indian Textile Journal*, Vol. VI, No. 61, (October, 1895) p. 6 (III).
[2] Tiwari, pp. 61–62 (III).
[3] Pearse, p. 120 (III).

considered one of the cities of India least under European influence, either architecturally or socially."[4] There was little
British investment; there were never many Englishmen in the
city; there was no higher education to speak of; the English
language was understood by few; and there was no English
press. Nor was there any great disruption of the traditional
culture, which some have assumed to be a prerequisite for
economic growth. Indeed the case of Ahmedabad confirms the
opinion of those who regard the extent of Western contact and
the extent of infra-structure provided as less important causal
agents in economic growth than cultural factors of a more
indigenous and long standing kind.[5] In the crucial early stages,
Western education was not needed; nor was Western law, as
there was already a well developed market economy based on
contract, indigenous systems of banking and insurance, a high
level of commercial morality, and machinery for the settlement
of disputes through the mahajans and seths. Though the railway was necessary to the large-scale growth of the textile industry, it will be noticed that the first mill was erected in
Ahmedabad even before the line reached the city. It must, however, be conceded that Maratha rule would have been poor soil
for economic growth, and that the greater security of British
rule provided much more favourable conditions for Ahmedabad's indigenous talent to express itself. It will not be denied that Ahmedabad's entrepreneurs, however traditionally-
minded, were awakened to new possibilities by what they
heard from the British officers and read in the press and that
some social change had already taken place by the second half
of the nineteenth century, limited and subtle though it was.
But the important thing is that Ahmedabad seized her oppor-

---

[4] Rice, p. 12 (III).

[5] Nor does the theory that withdrawal of status respect accounts for
the emergence of economic creativity in later generations seem to fit
the Ahmedabad case. (Cf. Hagen, *On the Theory of Social Change*)
(III).

tunity whereas other places which experienced far more Western contact did not.

Ahmedabad's advantages did not lie in foreign influence but were indigenous; they were not locational but social and moral. Her Vanias remained attached to their city, even in adversity; the Gazetteer noted in 1879 that while many Ahmedabadi merchants lived in Bombay, they did not settle there like some of the Surati traders, but returned for family ceremonies.[6] Ahmedabad had experienced and prestigious financiers and merchants and a skilled work force in her weavers and artisans. She had long specialized in textiles and was able to carry over much of her technique and acquired skill into the machine age. There was too, a dominant ethic of hard work, frugality, and money-making, which suited the rigours of modernization and met the need for capital. Seth Kasturbhai Lalbhai, Ahmedabad's leading industrialist and millionaire, has written about the Ahmedabadi temperament in relationship to the textile industry:

> It has a firm grip on the problems of life, with a dominant common sense to spot advantage even at a distance. On the other hand, it is sufficiently cautious not to be carried away by nimble imagination. As events have proved, it is an ideal temperament for an old industry like the Textiles. It does not require the bold vision of a Tata or a Ford, nor does it require the gambling instinct of a Rockefeller. It prizes are quite certain, and it can be started in a small way. But it requires an inflexible perserverence, an unflinching attention to each process, and unflagging effort to pass to perfection from one stage to another. In Textiles, one therefore never awakes to success; one works on to it, and if there are any people suited by nature to do it, they are the people of Ahmedabad.[7]

Moreover, the small plants put up by the Ahmedabadi entre-

[6] *Ahmedabad Gazetteer*, p. 295 (II).
[7] Rotary Club of Ahmedabad, pp. 31–32 (III).

preneurs did not call for any radical changes in behaviour patterns or social relationships in the city and hence they were
the more readily accepted.

Nor did Ahmedabadi society have some of the negative
characteristics which have hindered modernization elsewhere.
The situation in Ahmedabad does not conform to the standard
models of traditional societies, with their landholders deprecat-
ing businessmen and successfully persuading the rest of society
that business activities were anti-social and immoral. In Ahmedabad, commerce and money-making were not stigmatised but
were acceptable to all castes, and there was considerable mobility in Gujarat society, at least among the twice-born castes.
These statements would not be wholly untrue if applied to
many other places in India too; it is, however, a question of
degree. Nor were trade and finance divorced from production;
the sarafs had long been accustomed to financing trade and
industry. It is true that there was little interest in science or
technology and this would certainly have prevented an au-
tonomous industrial revolution, but this was not required in
the early Ahmedabad textile industry which could draw on
England's experience and expertise. There were firms to erect
the mills for others and there were Englishmen prepared to
come out to India, so technical knowledge was not required of
the promoters. The mills employed British, Parsi, and Hindu
engineers and the weaving masters were from Lancashire, generally selected men sent out by firms in England such as Platts
of Oldham. The buildings and technical side of the industry
were closely modelled on those of Lancashire. The availability
of British textile machinery and expertise by the mid-nineteenth century was of crucial importance in Ahmedabad's
modern transition.

Just as important was access to capital. Ahmedabad's merchants and financiers already had considerable capital, derived
from their traditional financial activities and from trading in

textiles, cotton, and especially opium. Indeed because of the contraction of former outlets in money-lending to princes and armies, the restriction of the opium trade, the decline of their insurance business because of better security, and the competition of the branches of the English banks, they now had more capital than they could profitably use in accustomed ways. The Gazetteer noted in 1879 that, as a consequence, interest rates were low in Ahmedabad; a respectable resident merchant or banker could obtain a loan for as low as two to four per cent per annum.[8] In addition, the city's merchants and financiers enjoyed the confidence of the people of Ahmedabad and could call on more capital from them. The availability of capital may be regarded, not only as an operative factor in the development of a modern textile industry in Ahmedabad, but as one of its causes also: the financiers were looking for profitable avenues of investment. Ahmedabad was not a seaport with a large import-export trade to absorb capital. It was, however, the largest city of Gujarat; it had a long association with textile manufacture, and it had a respected, indigenous mercantile class attached to their homes and their city. They stayed at home and put their money into textile mills, which offered the best return and promised the least disturbance of their old urban ways.

In Gujarat the profits from trade found their way into industrial enterprise and here a contrast with Bengal could be instructive. Of Gujarat, it was noted in 1901: "In a place like Ahmedabad, where there are many large traders, they would not like to invest money in land, having got other resources. There are very few banias who advance money in order to get possession of the land and become zamindars; there is no such feeling amongst the banias of Guzerat."[9]

[8] *Ahmedabad Gazetteer*, p. 68 (II).

[9] Evidence of Bhimbhai Kirparam, taluqdari settlement officer, to Indian Famine Commission, 1901, *Minutes of Evidence*, I, 881 (II).

In Bengal, on the other hand, those who became rich through trade tended to invest their wealth in the purchase of land. There had been promising beginnings in urban economic enterprise in the eighteenth and early nineteenth centuries, when Bengalis (some of them from the traditional trading castes, others not) became rich through acting as agents and employees of the British and subsequently invested their money in trade on their own account and even in industry, but later the Bengalis tended to retire from commerce and industry, leaving the field to outsiders. Today the Marwaris, immigrants from Rajasthan, have stepped in where the British left off.

There were a number of reasons for this difference between Gujarat and Bengal. First, there were the obvious differences in British interests and policy in the two areas. British firms dominated Calcutta more than they did Bombay, and once entrenched were able to keep a tight grip on commerce and exclude outsiders—in a way the Ahmedabadis themselves were able to do, or the dominant Gujarati and Marwari business communities do in India today. Moreover, the Permanent Settlement of Bengal in 1793 gave opportunities to invest in land through the purchase of *zamindaris*. The secure returns from land-holding and money-lending in the rural areas of Bengal contrasted with the risks of commercial and industrial enterprise in a city dominated by the English firms, with their inter-locking directorates and managers with contacts in allied banking and shipping concerns. In southern and western India, on the other hand, the land revenue was normally settled with individual peasants, not with landlords, and assessments were fixed for 30 years at a time and may well have been so high in some areas as to deter prospective purchasers of land.[10] British policy and interests were not, however, the only, or even the

[10] One-third of Ahmedabad district did consist of taluqdari estates, but most of the taluqdars were long-established Rajputs, Muslims, and Kolis.

most important reason, for the limited participation in the modern urban economic life of Bengal by the Bengalis themselves. Cultural factors are as relevant here as they are in the story of Ahmedabad's adaptation to the West. In contrast to Gujarat, banking and commerce had a low valuation in Bengali traditional society.[11]

Even after making allowance for location, timing, possession of capital, British policy and influence, and other advantages or adventitious factors, I have emphasized in this book the favourable cultural milieu in Gujarat. Although regional differences of this sort are often given little weight in general accounts of Indian history, they are widely acknowledged among the Indian people themselves and were recognized by the British administrators. In the nineteenth century, the Gujaratis (and not just their mercantile communities) were, of all the Indian peoples, the ones most favourably conditioned by their culture and history to take advantage of the new economic opportunities in trade and industry.

With this background in mind, let us consider the men who started the Ahmedabad textile industry. The father of modern Ahmedabad was Ranchhodlal Chhotalal, who was born there in 1823 in the Sathodra Nagar Brahmin community. He came from an old Ahmedabadi family, but not a commercial family. His forbears, on both his father's and his mother's side, had held high administrative positions under the Mughals and Marathas. The Nagar community has had a long history of intellectual and political achievement in Gujarat. Although Ranchhodlal was not the first of his caste to become rich through business, the Nagars have not generally been a business community. Under the Muslims and Marathas they were diwans, government officers of all sorts, teachers, and scholars.

[11] Cf. N.K. Sinha, II, 224–225, and Majmudar, *Cultural History of Gujarat* (III). See also the important articles by Pandit and subsequent comment by Acharya (III).

They are the most intellectual community of Gujarat and made themselves indispensable to the rulers of the Gujarat states.

Ranchhodlal joined the government service in 1845 after learning English from a tutor. He was in Customs at first but was transferred to the Political Department and rose quickly. He became *daftadar* (head clerk) in the Rewa Kantha agency and Assistant Superintendent of Pavagarh in the Panch Mahals district, that is assistant to the British Political Agent in that area and the highest post to which Indians were then admitted in the Political Department. But in 1854 he was suspended from the service for allegedly taking a bribe of 8000 rupees from the ruler of Pavagarh.

The incident of Ranchhodlal's "bribe" has become an Ahmedabadi legend; it is told as a secret to or withheld from visitors; it appears as a scene in Yashodhar Mehta's Gujarati play *Ranchhodlal*; and it would be appropriate to devote a little space here to the facts as they appear in the Bombay Government's thick files on the subject. Ranchhodlal was first tried before a Special Commissioner, Mr. H. Herbert, who ruled: "Not only therefore does the Commissioner hold the charge unsubstantiated by the proof adduced of it, but actually disproved. On every ground the Commissioner considers the accused so far as the evidence before him goes, entitled to an acquittal." But the Political Agent, Major Wallace, was certain that Ranchhodlal was guilty and brought charges of perjury and forgery against three witnesses who had appeared for him. These men were convicted and imprisoned but as there was no evidence to connect Ranchhodlal with their crimes, though he was the beneficiary from them, no charges could be brought against him. He was, however, dismissed and declared incapable of being re-employed in the public service in any capacity whatever. In reply to his many pleas he was told that the government had dispensed with his services "from its being satisfied that its interests will best be advanced by his exclusion from its employment." The dismissal was reported to London and the Court of Directors approved of it, saying that there was "no real doubt of his guilt."[12]

Ranchhodlal always denied that he took a bribe; his Gujarati biographer, Badshah, supports Ranchhodlal's story that he had been the victim of intrigue by jealous colleagues (quite plausible), and his English biographer, Edwardes, is equivocal. Although they never reappointed him to their service, Ranchhodlal rose to high favour and honour with the British in later years and came to be regarded as a man of the highest character and devotion to public duty. It is, of course, possible that he did take the bribe, knowing that it was improper to do so, and was extremely clever in his efforts to cover his traces but not quite clever enough. It is possible too that he or his wife, like other Indian and English officers before and after them, simply took a present from the ruler or his wife because it was a long-standing custom of the country—and the Nagars have, so they say, a tendency to live beyond their means, that is, in this case, beyond the meagre salary provided under the British Raj. But it is also possible that Ranchhodlal did suffer an injustice, unfortunate for him at the time, but most fortunate for him, and for Ahmedabad, later. The full facts will never be known. The British could not make a case stick at the time, nor can the historian now; and surely, after his subsequent four decades of service to his fellow citizens, Ranchhodlal is entitled to the benefit of the doubt.

While Ranchhodlal was still in government service, he became interested in the possibility of putting new life into Indian industry through the application of European methods and machinery. In the Panch Mahals he introduced, at his own expense, an improved method of manufacturing sugar. Whether he was thinking at that time of the industrial future of Ahmed-

[12] Political Department, Letters to Court 216/1855; P.D. 118/1853; 89/1854; 97A/1855; 126/1856; 127/1856; 171/1857 (I).

abad, of Gujarat, or of India generally, as stated by his Gujarati
biographers fifty years later, or simply of making more money
than he could legitimately acquire in government service under
the British, is not certain; probably both were in his mind. The
nature of the Western challenge to India was recognized early
in Gujarat, and Ranchhodlal, like Dalpatram, realized that the
invasion of Hunnar Khan would have to be repelled with
weapons like Hunnar Khan's. But Ranchhodlal is also said by
his biographers to have dreamed of acquiring great wealth, traditionally more a source of prestige in Gujarat than in other
areas of India.

About 1847, while he was still in government service,
Ranchhodlal thought of founding a textile mill. He obtained
information about English cotton textile machinery through
his friend Major Fulljames, Commandant of the Gujarat Irregular Horse, who was interested in industrial development.
Fulljames wrote to his brother in England explaining that
Ranchhodlal and his group of native gentlemen were "totally
unacquainted with machinery either theoretically or practi-
cally."[13] In 1849, that is seven years before the first successful
textile mill in Bombay started production, Ranchhodlal tried to
found a mill. He issued a prospectus, publicity was given to
the project through a local weekly, the *Ahmedabad Samachar*,
and the seths were approached. But they were too cautious to
put their capital into an untried enterprise and replied that if
cotton mills were profitable then Ranchhodlal could surely obtain all the capital he needed from the shrewd and business-like
people of Bombay. It was in 1861, after he had left the service
and after the success of Davar's mill in Bombay, that Ranchhodlal was at last able to start production. This was with the
Ahmedabad Cotton Mill, owned by the Ahmedabad Spinning
and Weaving Company, a joint-stock company formed in

[13] B. D. Badshah, *The Life of Ranchorelal Chhotalal*, p. 15 (III).

1859 with a capital of 100,000 rupees. Ranchhodlal's difficulties have become legendary in Ahmedabad. The first machinery was lost in a shipwreck, the second had to be brought by caravan from Cambay, the first English technician died of cholera and others had to be dismissed.

The other shareholders in the Ahmedabad Spinning and Weaving Company included the richest and most important members of Ahmedabad's traditional financial and mercantile elite—Maganbhai Karamchand, Nagarseth Premabhai Hemabhai, Hathising Kesrising (all three of them Jains) and an unidentified "White sahib" (possibly a Mr. White). Too much has perhaps been made of one writer of the fact that they rejected Ranchhodlal's proposals at first, to adopt them only after Bombay had shown the way and thus provide a contrast between "the elite norms of a traditional business centre" and "the modernization ethic of Bombay."[14] Surely it is more significant that an elite of long-standing and secure position should have been willing to listen to a relatively poor Nagar Brahmin outsider and ex-government servant like Ranchhodlal and trust him with some of their money *so soon* after the demonstrated success of Davar's mill in Bombay. It is not suggested here that the Ahmedabad mercantile community are bold innovators and pioneers, they are calculating and cautious, but rather that they do not deserve to be stigmatized as unenterprising, as they sometimes are by outsiders. Their ability to spot advantage even at a distance was tempered by a careful appreciation of business risks, a combination necessary for sound economic growth.

From the beginning, therefore, the traditional Vania elite of Ahmedabad participated in the mill industry. Ranchhodlal himself was always somewhat of an outsider, and this was true also of the second entrepreneur in the city, Bechardas Am-

[14] Pandit, pp. 316–317 (III).

baidas Lashkari. Bechardas was a Kadwa Patidar whose father
had been a financier and contractor having dealings with the
officers of the Peshwa, the Gaikwad, and the military department of the East India Company. The Kadwa Patidars had for
several generations engaged in industry and trade and possessed
much wealth in the city. Bechardas served in the Company's
army for a time and he helped the British during the revolt of
1857. In 1864, when the government disbanded the Gujarat
Irregular Force in which he was an officer, he decided to start
a mill. The Bechardas Spinning and Weaving Mill began production in 1867.[15] Originally a public ownership company, it
became a private company, then a joint-stock company. In
1877 Ranchhodlal, in collaboration with Maganbhai Karamchand, opened another mill, which was very capably managed
by his son, Madhavlal Ranchhodlal.

In 1878 Mansukhbhai Bhagubhai, a Visa Porwad Jain,
opened the Gujarat Spinning and Weaving Mill, and he and
his family later founded three other mills. There was opposition from the Jain community when Mansukhbhai started his
first mill, but this was soon forgotten though insect life was
surely taken every second as the raw cotton passed into the
machines. Economics proved stronger than principles here,
though it did not in the more blatantly objectionable trades in
alcoholic liquors, guns and ammunition, and animal hides; these
were left by the Ahmedabadis to Parsis and an occasional
Englishman. There were several other Jain entrepreneurs in
the Ahmedabad mill industry. In 1880, the Calico Mill, a steam
calico printing mill that had failed, was bought by Maganbhai
Karamchand, a Dasa Shrimali Jain of the old sarafi firm of
Karamchand Premchand, and converted into a spinning and
weaving mill. In the 1920s this mill was a pioneer in the machine production of fine cloth in India under the guidance of

[15] *Ahmedabad Gazetteer*, p. 64 (II); G.D. 56/1876, p. 86 (I); Evidence of Bechardas, *Report of Factories' Commission, 1875*, p. 137 (II).

Ambalal Sarabhai. The Sarabhai family is now noted for its wealth, service to the community, and patronage of and contribution to the arts and sciences. In 1895, Kasturbhai Manubhai (Visa Oswal Jain) promoted the Hathising Mills Company. In 1897, Sardar Seth Lalbhai Dalpatbhai, also an Oswal Jain, promoted the Saraspur Mills. His son, Kasturbhai, is the leading mill magnate in Ahmedabad today, a millionaire and a leader of the textile industry, the Jain community, and the city generally. But in the overall industrialization of Ahmedabad, the Jains were no more and no less important than their Vaishnava fellow Vanias. The ethic of the Jains was the ethic of all the Vanias, and indeed (in a less rigorous form) of many other Gujaratis.

The Vaishnava Vanias were not slow to enter the industry, and many were able to do so because of the profits they had made in the trade in raw cotton. In 1888 the Trikamlal (later, Maneklal) Harilal Spinning and Manufacturing Company was started by Harilal Harivallabhdas (Lad Vania), Parikh Trikamlal Jamnadas, Narottamdas Gulabchand, Trikamlal Bhogilal, and Girdharlal Amratlal under a partnership agreement. In 1889 Seth Motilal Hirabhai (Modh Vania) promoted a mill known as the Telia mill, in 1896 the Ahmedabad Sarangpur Mills Company, and thereafter nine more mills in Ahmedabad and elsewhere. In 1892 Balabhai Damodardas (Visa Porwad Meshri Vania), who had started as a clerk in Ranchhodlal's mill and whose father was a saraf's clerk, floated the Aryodaya Spinning Mill together with Mangaldas Girdhardas Parekh of the same caste. Balabhai and his brother Amratlal Damodardas floated the Ahmedabad Cotton Mills in 1894. Amratlal later promoted several more companies, and Mangaldas, in conjunction with others, nineteen companies. In 1893, the Manekchowk and Ahmedabad Manufacturing Company was promoted by Seth Trikamlal Jamnadas (Pancha Nagar Vania), a well-known saraf of Ahmedabad. In 1895 the

Gujarat Cotton Mills Company was promoted by Motilal
Ghelabhai, and the Ahmedabad New Spinning and Weaving
Company by Seth Lalubhai Raichand.[16]

These men were not outsiders. Except for Ranchhodlal
and Bechardas, they came from the traditional mercantile and
financial Vania castes of Ahmedabad. Before they became millowners they were, in the main, sarafs, cotton-dealers and mill
stores suppliers. They were men who remained within their
castes, faithful to their religious obligations and generous in
their charities. They were not immigrants from other parts of
India, like Calcutta's Marwari industrialists. Nor did they come
from a particular community which rose under the British because it was more adaptable and enterprising than others, like

[16] Most of the information on the founding of the mills is derived
from N. N. Desai, *Directory of Ahmedabad Mill Industry* (III), some
from S. Playne, *The Bombay Presidency etc.*, pp. 64–103 (III), some
from government files. Not every mill founded in Ahmedabad in these
early years is listed, no information being available for some. The following figures are from Desai, but may not be accurate in detail as
other figures are given elsewhere.

Year	Number of Mills	Number of Workers	Year	Number of Mills	Number of Workers
1891	9	7,451	1906	33	22,737
1892	9	7,829	1907	37	24,473
1893	9	8,147	1908	47	29,996
1894	12	9,448	1909	51	31,487
1895	13	11,084	1910	52	30,013
1896	13	12,037	1911	50	31,319
1897	—	—	1912	51	31,760
1898	21	16,134	1913	49	32,789
1899	26	16,964	1914	49	35,415
1900	27	15,943	1915	—	—
1901	29	16,887	1916	51	41,102
1902	30	18,831	1917	51	39,291
1903	30	19,132	1918	51	39,440
1904	—	—	1919	—	—
1905	32	21,585	1920	51	43,515

Bombay's Parsis. The Parsis have never been important in the Ahmedabad textile industry, though (to mention the earliest exceptions) Seth Sorabji Dinshaw Karaka promoted the Ahmedabad Fine Spinning and Weaving Company in 1898, and the Hitwardak Cotton Mills in 1900 (liquidated in 1901). In contrast to Kanpur, Englishmen have not been significant either. In 1905 a Kadwa Patidar, Seth Mafatlal Gagalbhai, together with an Englishman, Mr. Collinson Shorrock, and Mr. Chandulal Achratlal, promoted the Shorrock Spinning and Manufacturing Company, and later the Marsden Brothers owned a mill for a while. Seth Mafatlal's father was a dealer in silk goods. The Lewa Patidars did not become important till about the time of the First World War, and will be considered in Chapter V.

Those urban castes which had not engaged in business and industry in Ahmedabad in the days of Muslim and Maratha rule did not take to it now. Apart from Ranchhodlal, the Nagar Brahmins stayed in intellectual life and government service, and Ranchhodlal's family later withdrew from the mill industry. The Muslims remained humble weavers or gentlemen pensioners living in pride and semi-poverty. It has often been noted that their failure to take advantage of the opportunities open to them under British rule—for any British discrimination against them was less important here than their own lack of initiative—was of great significance in the modern history of the sub-continent. They trailed behind the Hindus in government service (except the army), in the professions, in commerce, and in industry. This was generally true of India as a whole (though pockets of Muslim enterprise were to be found, especially in Gujarat, including two cotton spinning mills in Surat started in 1861 and 1874) and it was certainly so in Ahmedabad, where there were no Muslim millowners and only one industrialist, Munshi Fateh Muhammad Fakir Muhammad, who started a match factory in 1895. Like the cotton industry,

this factory had to contend with the discriminatory tariff of
the B.B. and C.I. Railway: the freight for imported Japanese
matches from Bombay to Agra was the same as that from Ahmedabad to Agra, a much shorter distance. The British officers
praised this enterprise in an effort to encourage the Muslims,
whose failure to adapt to the new age had become obvious
during the closing years of the nineteenth century.[17] But the
lack of Muslim initiative in industrial development was not
surprising. Apart from the Bohora merchants, the well-born
Muslims in Ahmedabad had been soldiers and high officers, and
most of these lost their jobs under the British. Here they
showed no greater occupational inflexibility than the Vanias
or the Nagar Brahmins, who were able to maintain their positions; the Muslims were just less fortunate.

There was little or no obstruction of industrialization by
the mahajans. At first sight this seems surprising, perhaps, since
the English and European guilds are usually thought to have
been a brake on individual enterprise and innovation and hence
on industrial development. One Indian writer, doubtless with
this European experience in mind, has written that the new industrial ventures "were undertaken against the wishes and in
defiance of the big city mahajans of Gujarat," and the Gazetteer refers to "steam mills springing up in defiance of the guilds
and beyond their control."[18] However, no evidence, written or
oral, is available to support this view. In 1896, the leading seths
and patels of the Ahmedabad guilds told Hopkins that they
did not oppose modern improvements, and he did not dispute
it (though in 1820, Dunlop had referred to people being denied
the privileges of their caste "for the crime of having invented
some improvement").[19] A rather careless travel writer explained in 1905 that the guilds had not opposed the cotton

[17] Lely, pp. 94–98; Vallabhji, pp. 133–134 (III).
[18] Thoothi, p. 202 (III); Ahmedabad Gazetteer, p. 111 (II).
[19] Hopkins, p. 196 (III); Ahmedabad Gazetteer, p. 111 (II).

factories because their products came into direct competition only with the cotton goods of England (which was not so) but that they had become alarmed at the possible threat from silk looms and other new machinery.[20] The lack of hostility to the mills can be explained in other ways. The hand spinning and weaving of cotton textiles were not as important in Ahmedabad city as other handicrafts, particularly the various silk products and the dyeing and printing trades. In any case, the weavers could find employment in the mills, or, on the other hand, be thankful for the cheaper yarn which the mills supplied. The most important mahajans in Ahmedabad, the sarafs', the silk dealers', and the cotton dealers', had nothing to lose from the cotton textile mills. The industrialization of Ahmedabad was not carried out by a few exceptional individuals battling against the obstruction of vested interests and hidebound majorities. Almost from the start it commanded the support and capital of those who mattered. People did refer to Ranchhodlal as Ranchhod Rentiawalla (spindle man) but not in any spirit of hostility—that was kept for his sewerage and water-supply schemes. There were no Luddite riots in Ahmedabad.

Like much of modern industry in India, the Ahmedabad mills were promoted and managed by managing agents. Under this system, an individual, group of individuals, or a private limited liability company would manage a business on behalf of the owners and be paid by a commission on turnover or profits. But in Ahmedabad there were significant local differences. The share capital in the mill company was usually small, and the managing agent and a few relatives or friends would take these shares up and become joint partners in the enterprise, sharing not only the dividends but also the managing agency commission. The typical mill agent in Ahmedabad had more

[20] Curtis, p. 162 (III).

of his own capital invested in the mill than his Bombay counterpart. The public sometimes came in as shareholders, but more
often as depositors. Deposits, carrying interest rates of four
and a half to six per cent, were accepted by the mills and this
unique system provided nearly all the working capital. The
people of Ahmedabad were anxious to invest their money
profitably. They had confidence in the agents because they
were Ahmedabadis too, with long family traditions and a stake
in the city and in the mills which had absorbed so much of
their own money. Investment in the mills was widely diffused
throughout the upper and middle class people of the city. The
agents were able to raise all their share and working capital in
the city, without having recourse to outside borrowing at high
interest rates. Gradual but limited expansion was a corollary
of this method of financing the mills and they were of smaller
average size than those in Bombay.

One of the difficulties in the way of the industrialization
of other parts of India was the shortage of capital. The modern
capital market in India was not well organized. Much capital
went into money-lending in the rural areas and in Bengal into
the purchase of zamindaris, and there was little assistance from
the indigenous sahukars for industrial development. But in Ahmedabad, the sarafs' long association with the financing of
trade and industry continued in the new industrial age. The
new joint-stock banks, on the other hand, far from being a help
to Ahmedabad's industry, took capital away from the city. But
the mills could attract the capital they needed from the sarafs,
the merchants, and the public of Ahmedabad and adjoining
towns.[21]

Ahmedabad's merchants and financiers also enjoyed an-

[21] Evidence of Ahmedabad Millowners' Association to Bombay Provincial Banking Enquiry Committee, 30 Sept. 1929, printed in Ahmedabad Millowners' Association *Report* 1929–30 (III). For contrast, see
Jain, p. 46 (III).

other advantage in industrializing their city. They were all
Ahmedabadis of very few castes and many were related by
birth and marriage. For instance, the families of the Nagarseths,
of Hathising, of Maganbhai Karamchand, and of Lalbhai Dalpatbhai are all Jains and are related by marriage. In general, the
Ahmedabad mill agents cooperated, rather than competed.
Ranchhodlal presided over the opening of new mills. "He was
adviser-in-chief to all those who sought to emulate his success,"
and he started a mill for his son to manage.[22] Ranchhodlal's
successor as the inspiration of the mill industry was Mansukhbhai Bhagubhai, followed by Mangaldas Girdhardas, then by
Kasturbhai Lalbhai. Mangaldas Girdhardas, whose father was
a cotton dealer, worked for a few months as a storekeeper in
Ranchhodlal's mill, then set up a business in mill stores, in
which he was assisted both by Ranchhodlal and by Mansukhbhai Bhagubhai. After starting his own mill, Mangaldas helped
his caste fellows to start mills also, and like most of the other
millowners, he gave preference to them in employment in his
mills.[23] The lack of competition within the city helped the Ahmedabad mills to develop in the face of outside competition.
The market which they were taking from the hand spinners
and handloom weavers was large enough for them to remain
fairly united against outsiders.

The agents brought to the management of their mills the
ideals and qualities of generations of financiers and merchants.
They regarded their firms as family trusts to be conserved.
Kasturbhai Lalbhai has written that this survival of tradition
"has secured for the industry an identity of interest and pur-
posiveness normally absent from corporate management. It has
also secured a management which is ever watchful and which
is never tired of work. Altogether, it has so influenced the ideals

[22] Edwardes, p. 23 (III).
[23] B. G. Parekh, pp. 28, 66 (III).

of management, that, even to a casual observer the methods and practices followed at Ahmedabad appear different from those elsewhere, and the industry as a whole seems to be placed in a setting of its own."[24]

The managing agents not only had their relatives as joint partners in the agency and as shareholders in the company managed but also employed them on the business side as well. Thus the caste system and joint family system found new avenues of expression in a modern context, as they have done in many other aspects of Indian life. Indeed, but for the corporate spirit and confidence provided by these ties it is doubtful if Ahmedabad could have industrialized to the extent she did. No body of outsiders would have been able to attract such public confidence; they would have confined their entrepreneurship to a cosmopolitan centre like Bombay where there were more of their kind and a more fluid society. In the twentieth century these family ties were eventually to become a burden to some of the Ahmedabad textile mills. A far more sophisticated industry needed to draw on the talent of highly educated professionals, not always to be found within the family group, and the informal relationships within management had to be replaced by more formal ones with precise allocation of functions.[25] But in the less complicated early days, the joint family and caste systems were advantages to the Ahmedabadi entrepreneurs as they have been to other Indian industrialists such as the Marwaris.

It was important for their success, too, that the Ahmedabad mill agents lavished personal care on their mills. The old-style agent lived frugally, walked to work, stayed there 15 hours a day, employed a relative or two to help him with the paperwork, and knew every detail of the business, at least on

[24] Rotary Club of Ahmedabad, pp. 39–41 (III).
[25] See Rice (III).

the financial side. The business side of the mills was always an Ahmedabadi affair. The mills could not have afforded costly overheads in management and they rarely paid high salaries to outsiders. In general the strength of the agents was on the business side, rather than the technical, though one or two of them, such as Ranchhodlal, picked up a knowledge of that side too, sufficient to correct their engineers on occasion. Ranchhodlal visited his mill twice a day, entered every department of it, and conversed with the mill hands. He is said to have limited the number of his own mills lest efficiency be impaired through lack of his personal supervision. This personal touch was typical of the Ahmedabadi mill agent though not of his Bombay counterpart, who spent more time in his city office.[26]

Of course not every saraf and merchant of Ahmedabad became a millowner. Many continued in their old businesses, and profited from the expansion of the city's population after the growth of the mill industry. Some of the sarafs and merchants, including some of the most senior, such as Hathising Kesrising and Nagarseth Premabhai Hemabhai, limited their participation in the mills to taking shares or making deposits. Those who did take to the mill industry rose in the financial and social scale relative to those who did not. The profits were impressive and the failures few. Ranchhodlal's Ahmedabad Spinning and Weaving Company paid an average dividend of seven per cent in its first fifteen years.[27] Ranchhodlal became the most influential citizen in Ahmedabad. In 1896 Hopkins observed: "Not very long ago, at the time when Mr. Lely wrote for the Bombay Gazetteer, the Nagar-Sheth of Ahmedabad was still a very influential person, but he has already lost much of his power, which has been taken by a leading manufacturer, a man who does not belong to any guild, but by public

[26] Edwardes, p. 24; Pearse, p. 119 (III).
[27] G.D. 56/1876, p. 86 (I).

gifts and wealth, he has won in the business world a position
of commanding influence,—a fact indicative of the rapid passing
away of the old order."[28] But the Nagarseth did retain a position of great respect in the city. For instance in 1887 the
Municipality asked him to call a public meeting to cooperate
in the Jubilee festivities of that year.[29] And Ranchhodlal's successor as President of the Municipality was Nagarseth Manibhai Premabhai, who had previously been elected its Vice-
President.

By the end of the nineteenth century, Ahmedabad had become known as a modern textile centre, and if a gazetteer had
been written then, the mills, not the handicrafts, would have
been given most attention in the section headed "Industry."
Sometime within the next twenty years the city became known
as "the Manchester of India." Already by 1901 Ahmedabad
had 29 mills employing nearly 17,000 workers. Between 1901
and 1904, the mills of Ahmedabad produced eight per cent of
the total Indian production of machine-spun yarn and nineteen
per cent of the piece goods (Bombay produced fifty-seven per
cent and fifty-four per cent respectively). In 1937–8 the figures
were: for Ahmedabad, sixteen per cent and twenty-seven per
cent; for Bombay, twenty-eight per cent and thirty-four per
cent.[30] Most of the cloth was sold to local merchants (characteristically well-organised in the *maskati* mahajan) though
sometimes the mills sent it up-country to their own commission agents. Some yarn was sent to China and Japan at least as
early as 1889.[31] The Chinese market, which was significant for
the development and early lead of Bombay's textile industry,
fell away after about 1906 with the growth of the Chinese and

[28] Hopkins, p. 179 (III).
[29] Municipal *Proceedings*, 15 Jan. 1887 (I).
[30] Sastry, p. 23 (III).
[31] Bombay Government, *Papers Relating to the Revision Survey*, p.
9 (II).

Japanese textile industries. The local market was of greater importance for the Ahmedabad mills. At first the output consisted almost entirely of yarn and cloth sold in grey, not dyed or bleached, and the piece-goods were predominantly of the low-counts—coarse, heavy, and cheap. This helped the Ahmedabad textile mills to secure a strong hold on the north Indian markets and thus be little affected by competition from Lancashire, the loss of the market in China or Japan, or fluctuations in international trade.

The phrase "single-mindedness" sums up the Ahmedabad experience, the reasons for its success, and its limitations. In contrast to Bombay, where there were many export and import trades, there was only one important avenue of investment in Ahmedabad, and it was natural enough that the Ahmedabadis should have concentrated on textiles which had always been a specialty of their city. But this is not to say that there was no interest in other possibilities for industrial development, even in the early days. In 1882 Ranchhodlal looked into the subject of iron smelting, submitted samples of iron ore to an expert for analysis and had a few tools made from the samples for use in the smithy of one of his mills.[32] In 1884 he formed the Gujarat Coal and Iron Company Ltd. to develop any coal or iron deposits in Gujarat, starting with the Panch Mahals district, where there had been ironworks in ancient times. The directors and shareholders included the leading businessmen and millowners of Ahmedabad. Ranchhodlal wrote to the government: "Gujarat, as you are aware, is a rich and fertile country, its people are industrious and enterprising, and its resources are capable of much development, but in these days of progress and competition nothing can be done without steam, for which purpose cheap and good fuel is necessary." The scheme was abandoned because the Bombay

[32] Edwardes, p. 23 (III).

Government would not concede a monopoly of mining rights
over a wide area or for a specified number of years. The company had asked for a monopoly for 15 years of a tract with a
radius of 25 miles, but the government considered that this
would have been against the public interest as it would have
excluded other enterprises and the land concerned was forested.
The Revenue Commissioner had been in favour of granting the
concession because any discoveries of large coal and iron deposits would have been immensely important for Gujarat.[33]
As usual the British Raj had shown itself excessively cautious in
its attitude to India's entrepreneurs at a time when she needed
a bold approach to the development of her resources.

The Ahmedabadis also made several attempts to improve
transport to their city. The first railway in Gujarat, a short line
connecting Dholera with the sea, was built in 1850 and 1851,
on the initiative of Major Fulljames but with capital largely
subscribed in Ahmedabad.[34] In 1889 a committee was formed
for the promotion of a company to build a railway line from
Ahmedabad to Dholera. It comprised several of the leading
men of the city: Nagarseth Manibhai Premabhai, Bechardas
Ambaidas, Ranchhodlal Chhotalal, Mansukhbhai Bhagubhai,
Sarabhai Maganbhai, Trikamlal Wadilal, Syed Musamia Ah-
medali, Varajrai Sakarlal, and Mulchand Hathising. The line
was to pass through rich cotton fields and was also intended
to enable coal and stores for the mills to be imported more
cheaply than on the B.B. & C.I. railway. Although the Government of India was willing to make the proposed company free
land grants and other liberal concessions, the project came to
naught, possibly because the capital could not be raised for
so speculative a project—speculative because of the hostility
of the B.B. & C.I. railway company, which told the government that it would do everything it could to kill the traffic of

[33] G.D. 179/1884 (I).
[34] MacKay, pp. 223, 257 (III).

its proposed competitor, and because of the silting of Dholera's port and the Gulf of Cambay. In 1916 the Ahmedabad mill-owners were still complaining of the railway company's tariff policy which was designed to prevent the development of alternative transport facilities.[35]

Then there was the abortive project to dredge the Sabarmati to give Ahmedabad direct access to the sea. In 1894 the leading businessmen of Ahmedabad, including Ranchhodlal Chhotalal, Mansukhbhai Bhagubhai, Shambooprasad Bechardas, Lalbhai Dalpatbhai, Motilal Amratlal, Sarabhai Maganbhai, and Girdharlal Amritlal Desai, formed the Gujarat Navigation Company. They proposed to use steam launches and tugs to open up the surrounding countryside, bring coal and other commodities to Ahmedabad, and make it a great commercial city. They asked the Bombay Government for land-grants, a 99 year monopoly of traffic on the river, and a monopoly of the rights to remove sand from it thereby opening a channel for navigation. But the government regarded the project as "visionary and impracticable from an engineering and financial point of view," which it probably was, and nothing came of it. The Sabarmati, with its shallows and shifting course, has never been navigable.[36]

These experiences showed, however, that there was no lack of industrial enterprise in Ahmedabad. Nor was there any neglect of technical education. Ranchhodlal recognized that a purely literary education was insufficient to develop the resources of the country, or to help the Ahmedabad textile industry. Under his guidance, the Ahmedabad Municipality withdrew its contribution to the high school in 1886 and helped technical education instead. From 1889 municipal scholarships were given, to be held at the Victoria Jubilee Institute in Bom-

[35] R.D. 185/1890; 105/1895 (I); Indian Industrial Commission, *Minutes of Evidence*, IV, 452–453 (II).
[36] R.D. 105/1895 (I).

bay. In 1900 Ranchhodlal's son, Madhavlal, donated 100,000 rupees for the establishment of a technical college in Ahmedabad, to have an emphasis on the textile industry, and in 1902 the R. C. Technical Institute was opened.[37]

Ahmedabad's increased demand for raw cotton, foodstuffs, and a work force tied the surrounding areas even more closely to the economy of the city. Its hinterland was pushed further and further out. Towns like Viramgam and Nadiad became economic extensions of Ahmedabad and took their lead from it. Labour was soon coming from distant places in Gujarat and Rajasthan and raw cotton from south Gujarat. Ahmedabad yarn and cloth were being sold throughout Gujarat and Rajasthan and later in the Punjab, the Central Provinces, and the United Provinces as well. The development of the modern textile industry in Ahmedabad helped also to upset the balance of the traditional economy of the surrounding areas. Almost all the women in the towns and villages used to spin cotton thread. Coarse cloth for sacking and clothing was formerly woven by the Dheds and Muslims. The mills of Ahmedabad, together with those of Bombay and other centres, and the jute mills of Calcutta ruined their market and contributed to the rural impoverishment of this part of India. Poverty, in turn, stimulated migration from the villages and helped to provide a labour force for the new mills.

The labour force of the Ahmedabad cotton mills was more settled than in Bombay or other parts of India. In 1892 it was noted: "In Ahmedabad and Surat only does there seem to be a permanent class of workers who do not look forward to going back to agriculture. . . . Ahmedabad appears to be the only great centre of the cotton industry that possesses what may be called a separate mill population."[38] Most of the hands

[37] E.D. resolutions 1188/1886, and 1068/1900; *Reports on Native Papers*, J.D. 125/1889, pt. 3, pp. 200, 216 (I).

[38] *Bombay Provincial Report on the Working of the Indian Factories Act*, 1892 (II).

lived by factory work alone, and once they came to the city most stayed, at least until permanent retirement from work. The Ahmedabad Millowners' Association told the Royal Commission on Labour in India in 1929 that 80 per cent of their work force was permanent, that only ten to twenty per cent went to the villages for about a week during festive seasons, and that most of the workers brought their families to the city.[39] The more settled character of Ahmedabad's labour force and population as a whole, relative to Bombay's, was reflected in the proportions of the sexes in the two cities. In Ahmedabad in 1921 there were 765 females to every 1000 males, in Bombay only 525. But the large immigration into Ahmedabad had already brought about a reduction in the proportion of females from 1010 in 1881, to 937 in 1891, to 919 in 1901 and 848 in 1911 per 1000 males.

In 1921, 603 per 1000 of the city's population were born in Ahmedabad District, 128 in Baroda State, 73 in Rajputana, 54 in Kathiawar, and 40 in Kaira; the rest were born elsewhere. Of the cotton mill workers in 1926, 20 per cent were born in the city (including Muslim weavers and some of the Dhed spinners), 25 per cent elsewhere in Ahmedabad District, 20 per cent in Baroda, 10 per cent in Rajputana, 5 per cent in Kathiawar, 10 per cent elsewhere in Gujarat, five per cent in the Deccan and Konkan, and five per cent elsewhere.[40] The Ahmedabad Millowners' Association told the Royal Commission on Labour in India in 1929 that 80 per cent of their labour was drawn from within 50 miles of the city. The immigrants included many landless labourers, such as Dheds, and hand loom weavers like the Vankars, who could no longer make a living in their villages. These were regarded as untouchables and as they were unacceptable to the caste people in the weav-

[39] Evidence printed in Ahmedabad Millowners' Association *Report*, 1929–1930 (III).

[40] *Memorandum from the Government of Bombay to Royal Commission on Indian Labour*, 1929, pp. 1–7 (II).

ing departments of the mills, were employed in the spinning departments only. Kolis and Waghris came also, and Patidar weavers. Before about 1923, labour was not plentiful and the jobbers would go to the villages to recruit labour; they would, for instance, enter into contracts with parents of Dhed boys for their services for two or three years.

The conditions in the mills, although harsh by the standards of today, were not as intolerable as those in the early days of England's industrialization. There was England's experience to draw upon. The factories were better lit through their skylights, by the bright Indian sunshine. But there was often a foul and damp atmosphere because of the humidifying needed in Ahmedabad's dry climate. The hours of work for women and children were restricted by the factory acts of 1881 and 1891; although their provisions were often evaded by the employers, the horrors of England's industrial revolution were not matched in Ahmedabad. Still the hours of work were long. The mill hands worked from dawn to dusk (up to 13 hours and 20 minutes daily in the hot season); a half-hour break was allowed at mid-day and four holidays a month, usually Sundays, but on these days they had to attend to clean the machinery, which took three or four hours. The pace of work was not, however, as intense as in Lancashire. The Indian mills employed more operatives for each machine because labour was cheaper and less skilled. There were frequent individual breaks during the day, so that the contrast between the rhythms of their rural and industrial lives was not as marked as it would have been in Lancashire, or if Western industrial drive and efficiency had not been filtered through the screen of Indian custom and softened in the Indian way.

The mills paid lower wages than in Bombay which was a seaport with many alternative jobs available. Many of the mills could not have paid higher wages and survived. They were higher than could be secured in agricultural employment when it was available, though less than the income of a skilled handi-craft weaver. In 1888 the average wages of mill workers in Ahmedabad were 7–10 rupees a month, as against 3–3 ½ annas a day (or 5 rupees a month) for common labourers. They were paid by the piece. Compensation for injury was slight, when given at all, and medical care was only occasionally provided in the form of a first-aid box. Like others who were now exposed to the money-lenders, who were increasingly unrestrained by traditional social obligations, and who were protected by the British legal system, the workers were heavily in debt. This was due partly to the fact that they were paid monthly and up to a fortnight in arrears, and partly to heavy drinking and spending on marriages and other ceremonial occasions. The mill agents' contact with the workers was normally indi-rect, through the *mukadams* or jobbers. These people ensured that the machines were worked with full complements. They would offer inducements, such as tea or cash, to labourers to work under them. Close personal relationships were built up between them and some workers would change mills in order to follow a particular jobber. But the jobbers were able to abuse their positions if they were so inclined; they extorted money from the workers and favours from their women, and kept the boys in order with a stick. The children of the mill hands had no schooling and ran wild or worked in the mills. The housing of the workers, at first in huts, then in squalid *chawls* (blocks of single-room tenements with common facil-ities), was generally deplorable.[41]

The textile mills brought about a great increase in the population of the city both by providing opportunities for all within it and so checking any exodus, and by attracting many newcomers, workers for the mills, and traders and arti-sans to serve the expanding population. The populations within

[41] Evidence from annual *Bombay Provincial Reports on the Working of the Indian Factories Act*, and from Labour Commissions (II).

municipal limits rose from 116,873 in 1872, to 124,767 in
1881, to 144,451 in 1891, to 181,774 in 1901, to 213,727 in
1911, and to 274,007 in 1921, and the city was expanding
faster than the municipal limits.[42] The areas around the mills
began to look more like a vast overgrown village of mud and
straw huts than like old Ahmedabad. The settlement pattern
was not as haphazard as would have appeared to an outsider;
generally the workers lived with their kin in particular localities and would decline to leave them in order to be nearer a
particular mill. Still, the very rapid growth of these areas,
together with the haphazard locating of the mills and their
railway sidings, provided the Ahmedabad municipality with
serious new problems added to those it already faced in improving the old walled city as a place in which to live.

[42] The following are the figures adjusted for inter-censal changes of
boundary:—
128,505 (1872); 137,041 (1881); 159,366 (1891); 199,609 (1901); 232,777
(1911). *Census of India, 1921*, Vol. IX (II).

CHAPTER IV

Urban Problems and Solutions

In 1820 or 1850 or even 1880, Ahmedabad was inferior as a place to live in to what it had been 300 years before—for its poor people as well as for its rich. There was an obvious deterioration in the physical appearance of the city. The superb mosques and tombs were now neglected and tucked away from sight surrounded by shops and houses built right up against them. They were filled with dirt and weeds and, sad to relate, were even used as public conveniences. Except for Hathising's temple there were no new buildings of any importance; indeed not a single building of any architectural distinction was put up in the whole century and a quarter

of British rule. The fine, tree lined streets had been narrowed
to winding thoroughfares, choked by the traffic of pack animals, horses, and pedestrians. Gardens, which had once been
open to the public, had long since reverted to nature, and the
fountains were dry. The dust was bad as ever—after all, the
Emperor Jahangir had called Ahmedabad "Gardabad" (dust
city)—and the mud in the rainy season was worse since there
was now more obstruction to the surface drainage of the
city. The water-supply and drainage had been dangerously
neglected.

The historian is interested in changes in society, but it
should be remembered that the people of the city were at the
time more concerned with their human condition, their traditional customs, which remained essentially unaltered, and the
vagaries of nature. Of the last, the most serious were the earth-
quake of 1819, the floods of 1868, 1875, and 1927, the fire of
1877, the famine of 1899–1900, the plague of 1896 to 1907 and
1916 to 1918, and the influenza pandemic in 1918–19. Cholera
was an annual visitor to the city. At various times during the
century, failures of the monsoon rains led to scarcities of food,
and high prices brought distress to the poor of the city and
an influx of outsiders. Although it was now possible to do more
to mitigate the calamities of nature (as early as 1824, 250 people
were being vaccinated each month and Ahmedabad had received a modern fire engine from Bombay), God's will remained more important than the government's edicts.

That Ahmedabad was still a wealthy city by Indian standards was noted by all observers who commented on the
matter. In 1830 Dunlop said in a report: "The population of
Ahmedabad are the most thriving and prosperous I have any-
where met with," which was a tribute in part to his own earlier
administration, but still true enough.[1] In 1856 Buist wrote,

[1] R.D. 12/293/1830 (I).

"Ahmedabad is still famous for its gold, its silks, and its carved work, and its merchants and brokers enjoy a distinguished reputation for liberality, wealth, and enlightenment."[2] In 1866 Hope and Fergusson remarked that "its merchants are among the most enlightened and wealthy in India."[3] In 1885 Colonel Ducat referred to the "general affluence of the population" and "their good upper-storied houses."[4] But from long habit Ahmedabad's mercantile community lived frugally. The observation of Bernier and other European travellers who visited upper India, that the merchants of India concealed their wealth lest it be taken from them by rapacious officials, was not true of Gujarat under the Mughals, but it was certainly so under the Marathas. In any case, the Vanias did not put much store on ostentatious living, and indeed they were wealthy because they did not. The rich merchants lived, not in palaces, but in the pols among their caste fellows, though their houses might have more elaborately carved wooden fronts, "more picturesque than any in Nuremberg, being one mass of carving, figures, animals, trees, and flowers."[5] Their extravagance was to give feasts to their caste, particularly at weddings and funerals. As for the poor, Sardar Patel's observation, "our cities are a type of Hell,"[6] was not true of Ahmedabad in any period of its history before the late nineteenth century, when modern industry began in the city; and, bad as it was, Ahmedabad even then never quite matched the horrors of Calcutta or Kanpur.

Figures of house occupancy are in fact available for the nineteenth century, though they are undoubtedly inaccurate in detail. In 1824 there were 29,050 inhabited houses in the city.

[2] Buist, p. 62 (III).
[3] Hope and Fergusson, p. 3 (III).
[4] Ducat, p. 106 (II).
[5] Caine, p. 63 (III).
[6] Quoted in R. Parikh, p. 271 (III).

There were 32,221 in 1846, 33,329 in 1851, and 35,284 in 1872.
On each date, the average number of persons per house was
under four. In 1872 there were 31,405 houses "of the better
sort," and 3,879 "of the poorer sort"; the average household
was 3.35 per cent in the former, and 3.01 in the latter.[7] The
houses were chiefly upper-storied, built of brick and mortar
with tiled roofs. The contrast with conditions in other Indian
cities, where several families often share one room, hardly needs
stressing. There was, however, a decline in the *standard* of
housing in Ahmedabad after the mill industry began, though
this was masked by the statistics. In 1911 there were 84,375
houses for 213,727 people within municipal limits, but many
of these were just huts thrown together by the mill workers.[8]

But if the bulk of the people of Ahmedabad were ade-
quately fed, clothed, and housed in 1850, before the beginnings
of the mill industry, their environment still left much to be
desired, both by the standards of an earlier period in the city's
history and by those that were beginning to find acceptance
in the West after the exertions of devoted pioneers in medicine,
sanitation, and town improvement. It may be doubted whether
conditions were any worse in Ahmedabad in 1850 than in
many cities in Britain, but improvement in Britain came sooner
and faster. In Ahmedabad there was too much dust and un-
collected filth, too few public conveniences, and no proper
system of drainage for the sullage and storm water which
flowed into stagnant pools or along the streets and out through
holes in the wall. The streets were narrow and the pols, many
of them cul-de-sacs, were crooked, shaded and airless. Worse,
there were health hazards not even suspected by the people or
the English officers who presided over their government. The
improvement of the sanitation and water-supply of the city was
to be the work of many decades. Ahmedabad was to see re-

[7] *Ahmedabad Gazetteer*, pp. 293–294 (II).
[8] Municipal *Report*, 1910–11 (II).

produced the quarrels between improvers and conservatives—
"a reforming party and a 'muck party' " (as one English visitor
dubbed them)—that had occurred in England several decades
before.[9] There were the same financial obstacles. There were
the same heroic efforts of individual sanitary reformers, whose
enthusiasm was laughed or sneered at by their more "practical"
colleagues. The story is a familiar one, but as it has not been
told in an Indian context with its particular Indian difficulties,
some of them peculiar to Ahmedabad, it will be told in this
chapter.

As in other Indian cities, the problem of urban improvement was more complicated in Ahmedabad than in England.
The foreign rulers had to contend with differences in values
and customs, which compounded the usual ignorance, prejudice, and self-interest which urban improvers have to face. In
England, the reformers were usually right; they worked within
English society, and they understood it. But in India they were
not always right; their nostrums were not always appropriate
to the cultural patterns into which they would have to be fitted.
Then there were the political complications. The British Raj
was an alien government which was reluctant to impose heavy
taxation to effect unwanted reforms. The task of municipal
improvement became very difficult once it began to interfere
with the people's long-established habits and to be accompanied
by new forms of taxation. A complication was the introduction
of more democratic forms of urban government in the last
quarter of the nineteenth century. The government of the
city was transferred from the Collector and the old urban elite
with whom he cooperated to a group of politicians, drawn
from new business and professional groups and dependent upon
the electoral support of voters who were opposed to changes
in their urban environment and to higher taxation.

The history of urban improvement in nineteenth century

[9] Samuelson, p. 302 (III).

Ahmedabad falls naturally into two periods: first, that from
1817 to 1883, when the city was ruled by the Collectors—of
varying interests and abilities and devotion to their charge—in
cooperation with the leading citizens, the members of the traditional financial and commercial elite, and government servants. In this period many improvements were carried out, but
towards the end there was growing dissatisfaction. Municipal
measures began to interfere with the self-interest of the citizens
and there arose demands for a more popular form of municipal
government. The second period followed Lord Ripon's local
self-government reforms; the municipality was then more
popularly constituted but there was even greater controversy
over the sewerage and water-supply of the city.

The Ahmedabad Municipal Commission had a predecessor
in the Town Wall Committee.[10] The early history of that
committee illustrates the survival of the traditional institutions
of Ahmedabad, the community spirit which still existed in the
city, and the government's regard for the wishes of the people
and for their traditional usages. The committee originated in
the needs to protect the city and its commerce and industry,
and to collect the town duties, which were being evaded on a
considerable scale. The people of Ahmedabad had asked the
Maratha rulers to repair the wall, but in vain. Soon after his
arrival, Andrew Dunlop proposed that the British administration should do it, but the Bombay Government was not willing
to meet the cost that had been estimated by government engineers. Successive British officers reiterated the need. By 1825
the wall was in an even worse state than in 1817. The Collector,
Mr. A. Crawford, then proposed that a house-tax be levied to
defray the cost of repairing it, to be collected from castes not
from individuals, but again no action was taken. In 1830 Andrew Dunlop, by now Revenue Commissioner, pointed out the

[10] The account of the Town Wall Committee which follows is principally based on the documents reproduced by Boman-Behram (III).

danger "to a rich and defenceless city."[11] This time something was done. The leading people of Ahmedabad were consulted. They were opposed to the idea of a house-tax, associating this with meaner towns and with oppression and disgrace, and they suggested instead that the cost of repairing the wall should be met by a small increase in the town duties. This was acceptable to the government, and so the Town Wall Fund was born. They also suggested that the government set up a committee, consisting of the Collector and Judge, and that this should have the repairs carried out by contract, rather than in the British way of conducting public works through the government engineers which they thought too expensive. Dunlop agreed; he proposed that the Kazi and the Nagarseth be added to the committee and the government added the Acting Collector of Sea Customs in Gujarat. So the committee to direct and superintend the repair of the city wall of Ahmedabad was constituted on 22 April 1831. A small increase in the duties on certain commodities was made by Regulation XII of 1831. This increase was to be reduced after the work was completed to a level sufficient to meet the cost of keeping the wall in good repair. At first the Town Wall Committee let out contracts, but after finding the work had been badly done, they had it done under their own supervision.

The Town Wall Committee was not dismissed when the rebuilding of the wall was completed in 1842. In 1840 Mr. Giberne, Acting Judicial Commissioner for Guzerat and the Konkan, had suggested that the enhanced duties should be continued in order to provide for other improvements in the city, including a better water-supply and the watering of the roads to lay the dust and harden their surface. The government asked the opinion of the leading people of the city, and they replied, in a letter signed by the Kazi, the Nagarseth, and 41 others, that they thought that the duties should be kept at their

[11] Commissioner's circuit report, R.D. 12/293/1830 (I).

existing rates until certain further works were completed and then lowered to provide for the continuing expenses. Boman-Behram comments that their "brief and business-like" reply "evinces that shrewd eye for economy of ways and means which is the hall-mark of a very influential section of the Hindu community of Ahmedabad."[12] Significantly, the reply was delayed for several months because the people were averse to expressing their wishes during the absence of their Nagarseth. The works specified were the construction of a reservoir in the Manek Chowk, a *dharmsala* (a rest-house provided as a charity) for travellers and for feeding the poor, and a grain market, and the removal of heaps of filth outside the gates; permanent provision was to be made for keeping the walls in repair, watering the roads, conveying water to the reservoir, and feeding the poor. Except for the last, these proposals were acceptable to the government. The people attached importance to feeding the poor as a charity, but the government would not agree, saying that it would create a public rendezvous for the indigent and destitute and attract idle and worthless characters to the city.

But in general it was the government's policy to allow the people of Ahmedabad to have their own way in the spending of the funds, and the Town Wall Committee did consult representatives of the principal castes before proceeding further. After the repair of the main city wall, walls were built around the suburbs of Vitulpura and Saraspur. Vitulpura was outside the gate that led to the great southern road; if they arrived too late to obtain entrance to the city, merchants and travellers had to spend the night there, in danger of attack from robbers. Saraspur was a centre of silk manufacture; its inhabitants had contributed to the Town Wall Fund and had petitioned that they should have a wall too. In 1846 (or soon afterwards, for no records survive) the watering of certain city streets was

[12] Boman-Behram, p. XVIII (III).

begun, also the construction of a dharmsala at Vitulpura for travellers and a grain market, and the removal of dunghills from near four of the city gates. Other activities of the Town Wall Committee included, the maintenance of fire engines, the lighting of some of the streets, the provision and cleaning of public privies, the reconstruction and gravelling of roads, the filling in of holes, the removal of rubbish from the city, and the construction of police posts.

The final activity of the Town Wall Committee was, appropriately, in connection with the defence of the city during the northern and central Indian revolt of 1857. The anxious traders and financiers of Ahmedabad buried their treasure, and petitioned the Town Wall Committee to engage 400 watchmen to help the police protect the city. This force, consisting in the main of Rajputs, was raised and 21 of the leading men of the city advanced funds to the committee to meet the cost. The government was apprehensive that the mutiny of some of the Gujarat Horse and Second Grenadier Regiment would be followed by a rising among the poor Muslims of the city; and an auxiliary force of 2000 infantry and 150 horse was raised from "the dangerous classes," mainly to keep them out of mischief. After the arrival of regular troops in January 1858, the city was disarmed and an order was given that all private arms should be handed over to the government. Nagarseth Premabhai Hemabhai helped the government maintain communications with central India through a private messenger service. But just as it was not a turning point in many other parts of India, the revolt of 1857 was not a turning point in the history of Ahmedabad.

The evolution of the Town Wall Committee into the Municipal Commission was connected with the history of government policy on town duties and other restraints of trade and on municipal government in general. This book is not, however, the place to go into details of the history of this policy. Briefly, the Government of India was now totally opposed to all internal duties because they were restraints on trade and industry, and sought to do away with all of them by Act XIX of 1844. This superseded Regulation XII of 1831, which had given legal sanction to the Ahmedabad Town Wall tax. But the Bombay Government was able to rescue this duty on the understanding that henceforth it was to be simply a contribution to be collected voluntarily and "without dispute." On this basis it lasted another twelve years.

Because the British were opposed to town duties, they looked to other ways of raising funds for town improvement in India. In 1844 the Bombay Government published a draft act which provided for the formation of municipal bodies to be financed by various means, among them a house-tax. This alarmed the people of Ahmedabad, and 2146 people, headed by the Nagarseth, signed a petition to the government. They expressed their opposition to taxation for municipal improvements such as the making and lighting of roads and the police posts. They were opposed especially to a house-tax. They declared:

> The motive of government in framing this Act appears to be, to construct roads &ca. for the good of the inhabitants. But, Protector of the Poor, your intention may be good in trying to enforce a new practice for the welfare of the people, but we are not willing that a new practice should be enforced. To us it appears that the intention of Government thus to do good for the welfare of the people is in their own hands, but by introducing a new practice they only inflict a severe injury on the *ryots*. This is what we think. Therefore we are not willing that a new practice should be introduced.[13]

This opposition to any form of taxation but duties on trade, the imposts most detested by the government, was to persist into the twentieth century in many other cities besides Ahmedabad,

13 Petition, 25 Sept. 1844, (Boman-Behram, pp. 240–242) (III).

and was to be a frequent cause of dispute between government and people. Direct taxation was resented in India. In this petition the people of Ahmedabad went further. They protested against the continued collections for the Town Wall Fund now that the wall had been repaired. But this was inconsistent with their attitude only two years earlier, with their approval two years later of expenditure on improvements, and indeed with the subsequent voluntary collection of the Town Wall duties. Apparently the government's suggestion of a house-tax and other unfamiliar taxation had made them apprehensive and temporarily uncooperative. They were very jealous of their traditional rights. The East India Company was no longer simply following the local traditional usages and this was resented, just as it was in matters of religious custom. The language of the petition reflected the assumption of the people of Ahmedabad that the Company's government would be the sort they were accustomed to, only more just. The assumption was wrong.

A few months before there had been unrest in many parts of the Bombay Presidency, and even riots in Surat, over an increase in the tax on salt, which had been intended to replace the town duties and other restraints on trade. Afterward the Bombay Government became more cautious and did not proceed with its draft act of 1844. The Government of India determined that municipal charges should not be disbursed out of the general revenue of the state, and the Bombay Government added that there should be no assistance for the improvement of towns unless the inhabitants came forward with reasonable contributions. This voluntary principle was incorporated in Act XXVI of 1850 "to enable improvements to be made in towns." Under this act, the initiative for the establishment of municipal institutions had to come from the people themselves.

In 1852, after the Collector suggested that the town wall

duty should be put on a proper legal footing, 271 of the leading inhabitants of Ahmedabad petitioned to have Act XXVI brought into operation in the city.[14] They stated that although they were opposed to any increase in the taxation over the amount collected for the Town Wall Fund (then between 25,000 and 30,000 rupees per annum), they agreed to the Act being put into force in the city because it would enable a larger committee to be appointed to supervise the municipal improvements more effectively and be legally accountable for the monies spent. After some procedural delays the Act came into force in Ahmedabad on 1st January 1857. The thirty Municipal Commissioners were all appointed by the government, and comprised 14 government officials (European and Indian), and 16 non-official members, the leading Hindu, Jain, Muslim, and Parsi citizens. The first meeting of the new Municipal Commission was held on 23 December 1856, though the Town Wall Committee did not pass out of existence until 1858.

Four Europeans and thirteen Indians, including the Nagarseth and the Kazi, attended the first meeting of the Municipal Commission, with the non-official members in the majority. This was to be the pattern of future meetings; often the Collector (its President) was the only European present. Normally the Commission met quarterly, and routine business was transacted by a small managing committee of three (six from 1883 on) members, including one European. Over the years the Commission included, at one time or another, most of the leading citizens of Ahmedabad as determined by wealth, inherited social position, or public service. Some of these knew very little English and most of the work was done by a few members. The majority of the motions were moved by the Collector, by Nagarseth Premabhai Hemabhai, or (in later years) by Ranchhodlal Chhotalal and Bechardas Ambaidas. As

[14] Petition, 12 Aug. 1852, (Boman-Behram, pp. 274–275) (III).

it was not the policy of the government as such to interfere in the details of municipal administration, much depended on the Collector's zeal and interest in municipal affairs. Normally he was dominant in the Municipal Commission but occasionally his requests were refused and he was out-voted by the Indian non-official members.[15] The Commission appointed as its first secretary, Maganlal Vakhatchand, who had been the secretary of the Town Wall Committee and was the author of *Amda-vadno Itihasa*. It also approved an establishment of a staff, including four inspectors to enforce the municipal rules.

The work of the Municipal Commission was a continuation of that of the Town Wall Committee, but there was an acceleration of the process of substituting more rational, impersonal criteria for appointments and procedures in place of traditional usages and hereditary privileges. Already there had been a tendency to commute private rights to dues on trade to fixed allowances, to make appointments on the basis of merit rather than family, and to abolish rights such as those of the *marphuttias*, who were intermediaries between the merchants and the government in the collection of taxes. Over the years, too, there had been memorials and petitions complaining that such and such a right, preserved by Mr. Dunlop, had now been extinguished. There were more of these after the enactment of Act XIX of 1844. After the introduction of the municipal act into Ahmedabad, all remaining exemptions from town duties were abolished. When the Nagarseth, who had previously been allowed to import goods for his own consumption duty-free, complained in 1858 that "his dignity as an influential citizen" was affected, the government replied, "it is derogatory to a wealthy and influential citizen to seek to escape the payment of taxes which are levied from the poorer and less privi-

[15] For instance on 5 August 1874 the Municipality refused his request that the compound of the City Survey Office be watered at municipal expense.

leged members of the community." In the same year the
Municipal Commission resolved by 11 votes to 10 to allow no
exemption to the Gosaeejee Maharaj of the Vaishnavas, and
the same applied to the panjarapol maintained by the Jains. In
1864 it resolved that where there were two candidates for
employment, preference should be given to the one who had
passed the civil service examinations.[16]

Similarly there was a tightening of the city administration.
In 1850 a third, at least, of the potential yield from the town
duties was being lost through collusion on the part of the gate-
keepers, who were poorly paid and not properly supervised.[17]
It would be too much to expect that the tax was ever collected
in full since the opportunities afforded the gate-keepers for
harassment and petty dishonesty were too great. But the spate
of dismissals in the years after 1858, sometimes for slight of-
fences, suggests that there was a considerable improvement.
Inspectors, as well as gate-keepers, were frequently dismissed,
and it seems reasonable to believe that the municipal staff and
the public were being weaned away from personal influence
and bribery as the best way to conduct their business with
each other. At the same time, opportunities for fraud were
reduced through the simplification of the schedule of duties.
New municipal rules were promulgated, and there were fines
for making unlawful encroachments on public roadways or
for violating the building codes. These were imposed at first
by the Municipal Commission itself and then by a magistrate
on the evidence of the municipal officers.

Like other municipalities in India at the time, the Ahmedabad Municipality was not popular. This was, the Bombay
Government thought, "perhaps chiefly due to the exercise of
a too minute and vexatious interference with the domestic life

[16] Municipal *Proceedings*, 2 Aug. 1858, 1 Nov. 1858, 10 Feb. 1864 (I).
[17] Collector to Bombay, 18 Apr. 1850, (Boman-Behram, pp. 325–326)
(III).

of the people and a want of knowledge of and sympathy with their views."[18] Many people in Ahmedabad were against any improvements which would entail increased taxation, and they expressed their opposition in public meetings, through petitions, and in the press. Soon there were petitions of complaint that the people had been happier under the Town Wall Committee, that they were over-taxed, heavily fined for committing nuisances, and oppressed by the inspectors of a Municipal Commission, consisting of a few rich persons who were puffed up by the transient honour conferred on them by the government, but who were really statues for Maganlal Vakhatchand to play with—and more in the same vein. The complaints were reported on by the Collector and by the Revenue Commissioner, who disagreed in their assessments. The Collector (Mr. A. Rogers) stressed the useful work done by the secretary and inspectors; the Commissioner (Mr. S. Mansfield) thought some of the complaints justified. Some of the Indian Commissioners had complained that large sums had been voted for widening the principal roads used by Europeans whereas others, used only by Indians, needed repair more and were not as well lit. The government decided to take some notice of the complaints: the number of European officers on the Commission was to be reduced (though in fact few of them attended even the quarterly meetings), the better lighting was to be extended to all public roads, fines were to be imposed by government magistrates and not directly by the Municipal Commission, and three suburbs (Hathipura, Rajpur, and Madhavpura), which received no municipal benefits, were to be relieved from municipal duties, the duties were to be reduced and simplified, and the pay of the gate-keepers was to be raised in order to provide less temptation to fraud.[19]

[18] Bombay Administration Report, 1872–73, p. 323 (II).
[19] G.D. 23/1860 (I).

Ahmedabad was, for a time, a well managed municipality and considered a model one. It was noted for its good, well-watered roads. But in the late 1860's, retrogression seems to have set in, reversing the previous favourable contrast with Surat. Poor Captain Lyon, who came in 1869 to take photographs of Ahmedabad's old buildings, soon fled: "I did not think there was so dirty a town in the world in these days, it beats Naples and that is bad enough."[20] From 1869 there was again an improvement with the appointment of Mr. Borradaile as Collector. He took a close interest in municipal matters. A *halalkhore* cess was imposed for the removal of night-soil from houses. When there were petitions against this departure from the old method of private removal by *bhangis* (sweepers), the government urged the Collector to exercise the utmost caution, discretion, and moderation in the enforcement of the rules, so that the people of Ahmedabad would be shown that the municipality was actuated by a friendly, not a hostile, spirit towards them.[21]

But the city was outgrowing such paternalistic control. A Western-educated middle class was forming in India and asking for a share in government. Ripples of this change were felt even in such a centre of traditional values as Ahmedabad, though to a large extent through outsiders rather than native Ahmedabadis. In 1872 a committee called the Ahmedabad Association was formed to represent "the wants of the people" to the government. On one occasion it protested the fact that cartmen were compelled to carry officers' baggage. It was said in 1879 to be inactive, like other Gujarat political associations, but in 1882 it sent a memorial to the Bombay Education Commission. There was also an emergent press. In 1879, three weekly newspapers were published in Ahmedabad, one of 24 years standing, one of nineteen, and one of seven. The general

[20] Letter of 7 Feb. 1869, attached to G.D. resolution 815, 3 Apr. 1869 (I).
[21] G. D. resolution 2476, 20 Oct. 1869 (I).

tone of this vernacular press was critical of municipal taxation and interference with the habits of the people.[22] The politicians, although drawn from Western-educated professional people in the main, tended to exploit the conservatism of the public. The Western-educated did not, therefore, constitute the progressive force that might have been expected.

In 1873 a large public meeting adopted another petition, which had been signed by about 700 people, complaining about the invasion of their privacy by municipal inspectors, the fines for breaches of the municipal rules, the halalkhore cess, and the neglect of minor roads while those frequented by the influential were kept in good repair. It declared: "In their zeal to carry out favourite schemes of sanitation and reform, the municipal authorities utterly set at nought the feelings, the ability, and the circumstances of the people." The petitioners asked for elective representation in order to ensure more popular and independent commissioners. In the same year Nowrozjee Furdoonjee, speaking for the Bombay Association and the Poona Sarvajanik Sabha, brought these grievances of the people of Ahmedabad before the East India Finance Committee in London, and gave instances of high-handed control by the Collectors.[23] In 1874 the Ahmedabad Municipality was reconstituted a "City Municipality" under the Bombay District Municipal Act (VI of 1873), which superseded Act XXVI of 1850, but this was simply a formal change in the case of Ahmedabad. There was provision in the act for the Governor of Bombay to permit the election of the non-official members, but when the Nagarseth and a large number of other citizens signed a petition that this be applied in Ahmedabad, they were refused.[24]

[22] *Ahmedabad Gazetteer*, pp. 217, 311 (II); *Reports on Native Papers* (I).

[23] Petition 20 Jan. 1873, *Report and Evidence of the Finance Committee, P.P.* 1873, XII, 382 (II).

[24] Petition, 21 Jun. 1874, (Boman-Behram, pp. 423–425) (III).

Among the many petitions to the government about the acts of the Municipal Commission, there were complaints that it was guided by class interest. For instance, in 1882 a petition from the mahajan of Kapan complained that the taxation system discriminated against the poor, that the big seths were favoured because their spinning and weaving mills were not taxed, nor their raw materials, and that they, on the other hand, were harassed by the *peons* at the gates and their dutiable, imported cloth was dirtied. In 1898 two petitions complained of the levying of octroi on butter but not on the raw cotton brought in by the millowners.[25]

How much justification there was for these complaints of bias and injustice is difficult to determine. The Collectors could certainly exercise considerable influence and pressure on the Commissioners, if they were so inclined. The Commission was composed of government officers and of rich and influential citizens and they, in their turn, were able to influence the municipal administration to their advantage in minor ways. Octroi, like most systems of indirect taxation, did press rather heavily on the poor. Ranchhodlal Chhotalal wrote a minute in 1882 criticising its inequitable and vexatious character.[26] But it was the traditional Indian system of urban taxation and it was maintained, not because it favoured the rich but because it was acceptable to the people generally. Other forms of taxation were resented. It is true that from 1872 the millowners paid no octroi on their raw cotton, but this was on government instructions because the duty previously levied had mostly fallen on outsiders and had operated in fact as a transit duty. On the other hand, English yarn and piece goods imported into the city were subject to octroi, as well as duty at the ports. The rate of octroi was even increased in 1871 to help meet the cost of maintaining police, which was to be borne in future

[25] Petition, 26 Jul. 1882, G.D. 81/1882; G.D. 63/1898, pp. 21, 31 (I).
[26] Note of 23 Jun. 1882, attached to Municipal *Proceedings*, 24 Jun. 1882 (I).

by the municipality. This double taxation was explained on the ground that English cloth was a luxury and that it was better to tax the rich than the poor.[27] It is also true that the mills which were set up outside the municipal limits paid neither tax nor octroi. But sooner or later these mills were brought within municipal limits, and then the house and property tax levied in the suburbs included within the municipal limits, in lieu of octroi, fell more heavily on the millowners and other well-to-do people than on the poor.

In general the Commissioners, who were led, advised, and sometimes pushed by the Collector, performed their task with a sense of responsibility to the needs of, if not necessarily the wishes of, the majority of the people of Ahmedabad. But although they were not excessively ruled by partisan or class interests, they did seek to make municipal improvements within a social order which sanctioned inequality. There was a place for all, but not an equal place. They showed charity towards the poor and voted funds for their relief during food scarcities, but the low and exterior castes were to be kept in their place. Three Jains complained in 1863 that whereas formerly only Jains and Hindu Vanias had taken water from the covered reservoir built near their pol, now others of all castes had begun to take it, thus defiling the source and forcing the complainants to get theirs elsewhere. The Municipality responded by resolving to prohibit the others from using it. In 1869 several Dheds petitioned to be allowed to use the public privies, but were told that separate facilities would be provided for them if possible. In 1897 separate latrines were built for Bhangis and Dheds living near Rangila Pol.[28] When a new piped water-supply was installed in Ahmedabad in 1891 it was noted: "A few stand posts have been provided with push cocks for the use of the classes who are not allowed to draw water at the

[27] G.D. 36/1874; 44/1877; Municipal *Proceedings*, 18 Mar. 1871, 29 Nov. 1872 (I).

[28] Municipal *Proceedings*, 23 Jan. 1863, 4 Sep. 1869, 5 Feb. 1897 (I).

public fountains."[29] And in a list of municipal wants put forward in the annual report of the Municipal Commission for 1887–8 there was included: "the removal of low-caste and other such people from the city, for the reduction of over-crowdedness"—a survival of the old Hindu notion that the exterior castes should be kept beyond the city walls. The Collector commented: "Low caste and other such people are very useful members of society."[30]

One of the most important problems before the Municipal Commission was to relieve the congestion of the city's streets, especially on its main traffic arteries. In the seventeenth century, European travellers had remarked on Ahmedabad's broad, tree lined avenues. But in the eighteenth century, the streets contracted with the city and the old principles of town planning and administration were neglected. Thoroughfares became pols and houses and shops crept further out, encroaching on the roadways, which became ever more tortuous and obstructed. With the decline of good government, security became the first consideration. Encroachments were tolerated by the Maratha officers for financial advantage or from poor supervision or indifference. Mahipatram Rupram wrote of Ahmedabad in 1886: "In building it the main point aimed at seems to have been the security of life and property from violence. No regard whatever appears to have been paid to any regular formation of streets, roads, and thoroughfares. Houses were gradually erected agreeably to the social habits of the people and the political condition of the country, without any control or interference of the city authorities of the time."[31] With the

---

[29] Fardunji Cooverji, p. 12 (II).

[30] G.D. 13/1889 (I). "The low class people (*prakrti*) should be quartered outside the city," (*Devi Purana*, quoted in B. B. Dutt, p. 177) (III).

[31] Letter to Managing Committee, Nov. 1886 (Municipal comp: G.D. Resolutions, III) (I).

return of prosperity in the nineteenth century and the increase in the city's population, the congestion grew worse. There was now even more incentive to encroach onto the roadways because extra living space had to be provided for the larger caste communities which remained together, instead of moving into the less crowded parts of the city as would have been the natural response of a population not divided into castes. As Mahipatram pointed out:

> Families tenaciously adhere to the localities where their caste people reside on account of certain social and domestic advantages they thereby enjoy. Owing to this cause houses and building sites if there are any for sale are very dear in the most densely populated parts of the city even in very narrow and dark lanes. In Shahpur and Jamalpur within the city walls and in the suburbs outside there are large tracts of open and well ventilated spaces and building sites can be had there at cheap rates, but owing to caste ties and old habits and ideas the people obstinately refuse to leave their over-crowded and ill-ventilated localities.[32]

There was still much encroachment during the first fifty years or so of British administration; the process was reversed once the Municipal Commission took up the problem. The inspectors ordered the removal of any newly erected buildings or extensions for which permission had not been obtained. Permission was not given for protrusions beyond the street line, nor for roof projections within eight feet of each other across the street. Road widening was undertaken through the purchase, compulsory where necessary, of properties, or parts of them, where removal would make a distinct improvement in the minimum width of a street by removing a bottleneck. Panchayats were appointed to determine the amount of compensation where no agreement could be reached. But these com-

[32] *Ibid.*

pulsory acquisitions were still resented, particularly so in the caste-bound, spatially immobile communities of nineteenth century Ahmedabad.

Much of this resentment was directed at the city survey. It was begun in 1863 at the instance of the Collector, Mr. T. C. Hope. There had been no survey since 1824, land was rapidly rising in value and private rights were ill defined. It had been the practice for the Collector to sell by auction any piece of unclaimed land which was applied for, and though doubts about ownership did inhibit building in many cases, there had also been a great deal of construction on vacant lots to which the builders had doubtful titles. The flood of 1868 destroyed 9,566 houses in the city and rebuilding was accompanied by much encroachment. From 1873 onward, interested parties, supported by lawyers and the vernacular press, were petitioning and suing, impugning the accuracy of the survey, questioning its legality, and declining to pay for and accept the title deeds which were being prepared and which did not recognize the recent encroachments. This controversy was only settled in 1879 when the Revenue Code became law. The Municipality shared with the government the cost of the new City Survey Office and received the sale proceeds of the right of occupancy of most of the land resumed.[33]

The Municipality made several new roads through Ahmedabad in order to encourage a spread of settlement, relieve traffic congestion, connect the centre of the city directly with the railway station, and open up the pols. The cost of acquiring properties was offset by the sale of lots fronting the new roads. There were the Jordan Road (terminating in the new Premabhai Gate), the Oliphant Road (from the Ellis bridge to Asto-

[33] Proceedings, Government of India, Revenue & Agriculture Department, (Surveys), April 1882, B.11 (I); *Correspondence Regarding City Surveys* (II); see also Petition, 20 Jan. 1873, Finance Committee Evidence, 1871–1874, *P.P.* 1873, XII, 383 (II).

dia Gate), the Richey Road (from the centre of the city to the railway station—now called Gandhi Road), and other minor roads. This work touched the interests of many people, aroused great resentment, and was in fact no solution of the city's problems of congestion because it simply compressed the communities in the pols still further. In 1886 Mahipatram Rupram wrote:

> Our attempt to open up some quarters of the city by making new roads with a view to afford proper ventilation and lessen the overcrowdedness, have resulted in increased overcrowdedness in others, for the families whose houses were purchased, instead of buying building sites in the large open spaces within the city walls or in the suburbs outside, accommodated themselves in the other already densely populated quarters.[34]

The urban improvers had not taken sufficient account of the customs of the people.

Of fifty miles of thoroughfare in Ahmedabad in 1879, twenty-eight were fit for wheeled carriages, twenty were laid with limestone from the river bed and with metal, twenty-two were watered twice a day in the cold weather by carts and water carriers and bucket splashing from roadside channels. The main roads were well kept, but not the narrow by-lanes and pol streets.[35] Indeed the condition of the pols remained deplorable until well into the twentieth century. Their unsurfaced roads were not provided with storm drains and were dust traps in the dry weather and quagmires and sewers in the wet. The people in the pols seldom saw the sun and they never felt a fresh breeze. Of Saraspur it was said in 1888 that its condi-

---

[34] Letter to Managing Committee, Nov. 1886 (Municipal comp: G.D. Resolutions III) (I).

[35] *Ahmedabad Gazetteer*, p. 313 (II); N.D. Municipalities Report, 1878–79 (G.D. 38/1879) (I).

tion "would disgrace the most uncivilized hamlet in India."[36]
The Municipality began to metal the pol roads in 1886, but
this process was slow because road metal was scarce and expensive near the city. Ahmedabad retained its reputation for
being a city of dust and mud.

Before we come to the two most expensive and, as it
turned out, most controversial problems—the provision of a
piped water-supply and of underground drainage—some other
activities of the Municipal Commission should be noticed. It
maintained fire engines. The main streets of the city were lit
by oil lamps; kerosene was used from 1868. The lighting and
watering of the roads, the scavenging, and the collection of
taxes, were normally carried out by the Commission's own employees, though at other times through contractors (Hindus
or Parsis). When prominent people, chiefly Englishmen—roy-
alty, governors, and the like—visited Ahmedabad, the Municipality arranged receptions and addresses of welcome and had
the roads and public buildings illuminated. From 1862 it contributed to the cost of the vernacular and English schools in
the city. Vaccinators were paid and hospitals, dispensaries, and
the lunatic asylum were maintained or supported. In 1882 the
Hathising and Premabhai Hospital, the Bechardas dispensary,
the Ranchhodlal dispensary, the Raipur dispensary, and the
Kagdapith leper hospital existed—several of these institutions
named after wealthy benefactors.[37] From 1875 it had a full-
time health officer. In 1872 the repair of the Kankaria was undertaken; this was a reservoir, a regular polygon of 34 sides,
covering 72 acres with an adjacent garden, which had been

[36] Collector, 11 Sept. 1888, G.D. 13/1889 (I).
[37] Under Bombay Act II of 1862, authority had been given municipalities to apply a portion, not exceeding 25 per cent, of their annual
revenue to the construction and support of dispensaries, hospitals
and schools, and under the Public Works Loan Act of 1871 they could
borrow in order to carry out extensive works to improve the public
health and convenience.

first completed in 1451. It is now once again a favourite pleasure resort of the people of Ahmedabad and there is a delightful
children's park overlooking it. In 1877 the Municipality laid
down a public garden near the Karanj (in Muslim days a pond
and fountain) in the centre of the city. At the request of the
Collector, the Municipality met half the cost of restoring a pre-
carious pillar of Rani Rupmati's mosque, one of the city's architectural gems. It helped pay for the construction of both the
first (1870) and second Ellis bridge (1892). It let two new
gates into the city wall and constructed municipal offices and a
vegetable market, which the people would not use. It was wor-
ried by the pollution of the air, soil, and water of the city from
"dangerous and offensive trades" such as dyeing, tanning, pot-
tery, and tile making, and though reluctant to interfere with
their ancestral occupations, it encouraged these people to move
out by providing them with land outside the walls. In 1880 a
Bombay Government officer wrote: "No-one who knew what
Ahmedabad was like, not many years ago, could be but struck
with the wonderful improvement of late years."[38]

In Mughal days the city had been supplied with water by
aqueducts and wells, including several attractive step-wells.
But long before British times the aqueducts had fallen into
disrepair, and the people of Ahmedabad obtained their water
from wells, the river, and household cisterns containing rain-
water collected from the roofs. In 1845, the leading citizens
agreed that money should be spent from the Town Wall Fund
for water to be brought to the Manek Chowk, and four years
later a piped supply was provided. Water was pumped from
the river by Persian wheels turned by bullocks (steam pumps
were substituted in 1866) into a 52 foot tower, filtered through
vegetable charcoal and gravel, and brought through a masonry
guarded eight inch earthern pipe into the heart of the city and

[38] N.D. Municipalities Report, 1879–80 (G.D. 62/1881) (I).

there distributed from seventeen iron stand-pipes, ten masonry reservoirs, and a number of connections to private property. But within a few years this supply was insufficient, even to put out the frequent fires in the city. From 1874 the Collector, Mr. Borradaile, repeatedly drew the attention of the Bombay Government to the city's high death-rate (45.76 per thousand) and to its need for a safe water-supply. In 1875 Dr. T. G. Hewlett, Sanitary Commissioner to the Bombay Government, wrote a long report on Ahmedabad in which he exposed its "eminently dangerous state" and urged the government to make immediate improvements. The Collector was anxious to carry out one or other of several schemes for improving the water-supply suggested by government officers, but there was delay on account of the cost and disagreement over which scheme was best.[39]

A systematic investigation, undertaken in 1885 by Colonel Walter Ducat, R.E., Consulting Sanitary Engineer to the Government of Bombay, showed that the water-supply was even worse than had been believed. The pumped water turned out to be the worst of all; it was found by the chemical analyst to the government to be "quite unfit for potable purposes." Hydraulic engineering had still been in its infancy in 1849, even in Europe, and the amount of technical expertise available for India had been limited. The pumping station had been located at the southwestern corner of the city, presumably because the river was deepest there. This was below the principal ravine carrying off the surface water of the city. "A worse site, from a sanitary point of view, could not have been found for a pumping station along the whole river frontage of Ahmedabad." In 1884 the course of the river in the dry season had shifted to the other side of the main sandy bed, and although a channel had been cut across the sand, stagnant water contaminated by the

[39] Report on town duties by J. Langford, R.D. 106/1069/1839 (I); Boman-Behram, p. 146 (III); Dr. Hewlett's report, G.D. 78/1875; G.D. 97/1876 (I); *Ahmedabad Gazetteer*, p. 314 (II).

drainage of the city was being pumped into Ahmedabad through the inadequate filters and settling tanks. With it came cholera, which always broke out first among those who used the municipal water-supply. Little better was the water from the wells, because the sub-soil water was contaminated by the drainage of the city, particularly its cesspools. Even the water drawn by hand from the Sabarmati was often contaminated. Thousands of people lined the river over a frontage of two miles, washing and dyeing clothes, cleaning animals, and burning bodies. Frequently the water was not drawn from the moving stream but from stagnant pools.

The least impure water was that supplied by the 8000–9000 household *tankas* (cisterns) in the better houses. These often dated from the time of Muslim rule. They were carefully constructed brick reservoirs under the floor of a room or courtyard, lined with plaster and filled with rain-water by channels or pipes from the roof. The precautions taken to ensure the purity of this water are illustrative of the standards of urban life which had existed in old Ahmedabad before the decline of the eighteenth and nineteenth centuries. The water from the roof could be directed at will into the cistern or not, and was not so directed until the roof was clean; the water from the part of the roof where people walked about was never taken; and the mouth of the cistern protruded above the floor level, so no water could accidentally flow into it, and was kept constantly closed. In most cases this water would have given excellent results under chemical analysis. Some of the cisterns were old, cracked, and contaminated, but in general they provided the best water-supply available in the city.[40]

Like the water, the drainage and sewage disposal of the city were also unsatisfactory, not only by modern Western standards but by those of old Ahmedabad as well. There can,

[40] Ducat, pp. 4–17 (II).

of course, be no real comparison between the standards of the sixteenth and twentieth centuries—a medieval city in India, or in Europe, was a noisome place—but the Indian sun and the bhangis, who traditionally served a group of households, helped. In Ahmedabad, too, there was the ancient *khalkuva*. In 1885 there were 7,644 of these brick cesspools. They were usually in the street close to the house and up to twenty-five feet deep. They took the sullage water from the houses and liquid from the household privies which were cleaned daily by the bhangis. The theory was that these liquids would then seep into the sub-soil water and be carried away, which indeed most of them were, but into the river and thence back into the municipal water-supply. The khalkuva was a product of a pre-scientific age. Just as people who are not germ conscious will think a plate hygienic if it has been wiped clean, so the people of Ahmedabad thought their sanitary arrangements satisfactory because nothing remained on the surface to give offence. But over the years the sub-soil had become badly water-logged and polluted.[41] Foul gases entered the houses and damp crept up their walls. Moreover, the khalkuvas were not used in the rainy season lest they over-flow, nor by the Jains because insect life was generated and killed in them. There were additional health hazards for the Muslims because many of them had khalkuva privies inside their houses to safeguard the *pardah* (seclusion) of their women. But the majority of houses had no khalkuvas at all. In their case the dirty water was supposed to be put into large iron pans placed in the streets or courtyards of the houses from whence it was removed daily; more often it was simply thrown on to the street. The only drains in the city were the storm water gutters along the main roads. Many of these were not paved and had to be cut at the beginning of each monsoon.

[41] This pollution of the sub-soil and resulting unhealthiness is, incidentally, one of the possible explanations of the shifts in location of Indian cities in the past.

Some improvements had been made before Ducat's time. In 1877 the Municipality prohibited the construction of deep well privies and in 1879 it closed all existing ones, involving itself in considerable expense and litigation. After 1870 a halalkhore cess was imposed on the owners of privies in the main walled city, and this was extended to Saraspur in 1884 and to all other suburbs within the city limits in 1890. Household, municipal, and panch (pol) privies were cleaned daily by municipal servants, and from 1884 onward the night-soil was carried to tramway carts outside the city. These took it to a depot 2½ miles away, where it was manufactured into poudrette and sold to cultivators. But this was just a start.

In Ducat's words: "As an example to the sanitary engineer, of what should not be done, Ahmedabad is invaluable; it is absolutely impossible to exaggerate the errors that have been and are still being committed; the earth, the air, and the water are all poisoned." It was no wonder, he concluded, that the death-rate in Ahmedabad (averaging 45.2 per thousand in 1880–4, and rising) was one of the highest of cities in the world for which statistics were available, far higher than others in the Bombay Presidency, and even than Calcutta, which had a greater population density.[42]

The task of improving these conditions fell to a reconstituted Municipal Commission controlled by Ahmedabadis themselves. Here it is necessary to refer once again to the history of local self-government in India generally. In 1882, on the initiative of the Liberal Viceroy, Lord Ripon, the Government of India adopted the principle that there should be an expansion of local self-government in India. The provincial governments were urged to have their local bodies popularly elected and given more autonomy, not because it was supposed

[42] Ducat, p. 22 (II). There was much dispute about the normal death-rate in Ahmedabad, which was put at over 50 per thousand by Ranchhodlal and government officers, but at under 40 by the commissioners who opposed sanitary reform.

that the work would be better done in this way but as "an
instrument of political and popular education." The Government of India conceded that in the Bombay Presidency the
municipal law was perhaps the best in India and that the municipal bodies were functioning well there, but still asked for
changes. The Bombay Government thought that the central
government's insistence on "very radical" measures of self-
government was "somewhat premature." Were the personal
supervision of government officers abruptly withdrawn, there
would be a retrogression in such matters as the progressive substitution of direct taxation for octroi, strict conservancy and
scavenging instead of habits of primitive filth, and the education of females and of the lower castes. It agreed to "tenta-
tive and experimental action" only. In future at least half the
members of the city municipalities (excluding the President)
were to be elected; the President was still to be nominated by
government, but where possible he was to be a private gentleman, and his executive power was to be extended to the general body. The Ahmedabad Municipality was relieved of the
policing charges laid on it in 1871, and instead was to pay for
the establishment and maintenance of the middle and primary
schools, though these were still to be supervised by the Education Department of the Bombay Government.

The first elections were held in Ahmedabad in March
1883. They were held by ward, and not by caste. This was in
accordance with the view of the majority of prominent citizens
consulted. The Revenue Commissioner had been afraid that
under this system it would be difficult to ensure a fair representation of all interests and communities, especially the poorer
people and the Muslims. His fear was justified by the result of
the first election. Four lawyers, four Indian officers of the Education Department, one merchant (all these Hindus or Jains),
and three Parsis (two of them businessmen) were elected. The
Muslims, the Patidars, and the Vaishnava Vanias, failed to return a single candidate. Canvassing had won the day in Ah-

medabad's first experience of modern politics and traditional standing had taken second place. In later elections, the complaint was heard that men of reputation and character would not deign to stand and canvass for votes, while those who were elected had appealed to the most sordid motives of the electors. But the government was able to correct this to some extent by using its power of nomination to appoint outstanding citizens and representatives of minority communities to the Municipal Commission.[43]

The government appointed Ranchhodlal Chhotalal to be the first non-official Chairman of the Managing Committee. This followed his election by the new Municipal Commission. It is interesting that the Commission first resolved to appoint the Nagarseth of the city, Premabhai Hemabhai, who declined because of old age.[44] They passed over Bechardas Ambaidas, C.S.I., the millowner and former member of the Bombay Legislative Council, who no longer commanded the confidence of the Collector, Mr. J. B. Richey, either, chiefly because of his evasion of the conditions attached to his purchase of a piece of ground from the government. In Mr. Richey's opinion, he no longer held his former weight among the people.[45] Ranchhodlal had proven his capacity in business and had also taken a prominent and sensible part in the proceedings of the Municipal Commission to date. The decision to make him Chairman, and, in 1885, President, was a most fortunate one. Ultimately it belied the Bombay Government's fears that the extension of

[43] F.D. 6/1882; 8/1882; 48/1883; 53/1883; 54/1883; 56/1883; 58A/1883; 58B/1883; G.D. 10/1890 (I). The number of commissioners was altered from time to time, and so was the franchise, though it was confined to categories of property owners, tax payers, and professional men.

[44] Municipal *Proceedings*, 10 Jul. and 24 Oct. 1883 (I). Kavasji Mancherji, Mahipatram Rupram, Abaji Vishnu Kathavate, and Rattanlal Trimbuklal voted for Bechardas.

[45] Collector to Commissioner (confidential), 23 Mar. 1883, F.D. 53/1883 (I).

local self-government would mean a retrogression in municipal improvement. Nevertheless Ranchhodlal was to quarrel
with the elected members, and their obstruction of his plans
for improving the city showed that there was much justification for these fears. Without Ranchhodlal's vision, moral cour-
age, and perseverance, the improvement of the sanitation and
water-supply of Ahmedabad would have been further delayed.

In December 1883, soon after his appointment as Chairman, Ranchhodlal wrote a memorandum listing the needs of
the city. The Sanitary Commissioner for the Bombay Government described it as "a remarkable document for a native
gentleman to have written." The list included better water and
drainage, new thoroughfares, more open spaces, better hospitals, the encouragement of people to live outside the wall,
and a ban on selling further land for building in the crowded
parts of the city. Ranchhodlal wrote: "The most important
duty of the Municipality is to look after the public health."[46]
He visited the Calcutta Exhibition to gather information about
these problems, consulted all the experts he could, and sought
the approval of the Municipality and the government first, to
raise a loan to carry out improvements in the sanitation and
water-supply of the city, especially underground drainage and
piped water, and second, for increases in municipal taxes to
meet the repayments. He was very tactful, persuasive, and te-
nacious. He wrote: "We know that the good people of Ahmedabad try their best to save any animal life and if they
realise the fact that as many as 2,500 human lives can be saved
every year by adopting proper measures of water supply and
drainage they will, I think, be quite willing to sacrifice anything in their power."[47] He was to be disappointed by his fellow
citizens.

The proposal for increased taxation was more than any-

[46] Memorandum, 8 Dec. 1883, G.D. 104/1884 (I).
[47] Memorandum, 24 Mar. 1886 (*Compilation* Water-Works II) (I).

thing else responsible for the hostility that Ranchhodlal now had to face from a very large section of the people of Ahmedabad. Agitation was whipped up by the local press and by several of the elected commissioners. In 1885 Mr. Crawley-Boevey, the acting Collector, referred to a small but influential party headed by Rao Saheb Mahipatram Rupram, C.I.E., which was determined to resist measures expected to entail increased taxation. In his opinion, Mahipatram and other officers of the Education Department had improperly used their official positions in this agitation. The government declined to interfere as long as Mahipatram's work at the Training College was satisfactory, which it was.[48] Other prominent citizens who opposed Ranchhodlal's schemes for improvement were Kavasji Mancherji Karanjawala, Bechardas Ambaidas, the Padshahi Diwan Mirza Najaf Ali Khan Valade Mirza Nawab, Desaibhai Kalidas Vakil, Ardeshir Kavasji Karanjawala, Maganlal Sarupchand, and Keshavlal Motilal. This was a mixed bag. It included people who were distinguished for their service to the city and the cause of social reform and improvement. Their motives were various. Opposition to increased taxation was especially important. Personal jealousy of Ranchhodlal was there too. So were demagogy, opportunism, self-seeking and vanity. Religious prejudice played a part, not so much with the leaders, but with many of those who followed. This was because the piped water-supply would be accessible to all castes; at first the Brahmins and Vaishnava Vanias would not use piped water and even today there are some Vaishnavas in Ahmedabad who will not. Finally, there were the beliefs that an increased water-supply would add to the dampness of the city's soil, leading to an increase in fever, and that underground drainage was unpractical, doctrinaire, still in the experimental stage elsewhere (an argument with appeal to the cautious Ah-

[48] Acting Collector to Commissioner, 12 Nov. 1885, G.D. Resolution, 16 Dec. 1885, G.D. 84/1885; E.D. Res. 9 Apr. 1886, G.D. 62/1886 (I).

medabadis), and dangerous to health. It was argued that other improvements should have priority, especially in the pols.

A fierce controversy ensued.[49] Both sides drew on outside opinions and wrote long memoranda in defence of their views. Ranchhodlal even wrote to Florence Nightingale to obtain her recommendation of underground drainage. Petitions against the water-supply and drainage schemes were adopted at public meetings and signed by thousands of people. Ranchhodlal was accused of having a reckless disregard for the health and pocketbooks of the people of Ahmedabad. He was pelted in the streets. Mahipatram Rupram wrote that the air in the narrow and ill-ventilated streets would be poisoned by the gases emerging from the openings in the underground drains. The Bombay Government supported Ranchhodlal, but when he brought Colonel Ducat and Dr. Hewlett especially to Ahmedabad to talk to the Commissioners, his colleagues stayed away and the meeting had to be adjourned for want of a quorum. Instead his opponents solicited the advice of a former Collector, Sir Theodore Hope, and were encouraged when he replied with a memorandum which urged Ahmedabad "to have nothing to do with underground drainage," since it was costly, still in its experimental stage in India with mistakes still being made even in England, and "too far advanced for the present stage of average intelligence and civilisation of the population of towns in the Bombay mofussil."[50] Because the local press was against Ranchhodlal, the Municipality published *The Ahmedabad Municipal Record*, in English and Gujarati, "to communicate Municipal information to the public and make them take interest in Municipal affairs, to counteract the effect of misrepre-

---

[49] The information on this controversy was derived from the Municipal *Proceedings;* the *Compilation* Water-Works; G.D. 65/1887; 104/1887; 115/1887; 82A/1888; 103/1889; the *Reports on Native Papers;* and the Municipality's *Compilation* of G.D. resolutions (I).

[50] Memorandum, 25 Oct. 1886, *Compilation* Water-Works II (I).

sentation and prepare the people to approve the action of the Municipality and to cooperate in carrying out sanitary reforms calculated to promote their health and comfort and lessen the causes of disease and deaths as far as our means and knowledge will permit."[51]

Finally the Commissioners did agree to an improved water-supply scheme, a modification of one of Ducat's alternative schemes, though a majority of the elected members wanted an even cheaper scheme. This supplied good water to the city from 1891 and elicited a rush for house connections. But they refused to carry out Ducat's proposals for underground drainage and resolved instead that the sullage water of the city should be collected in carts. Ranchhodlal suggested that the Bombay Government allow this scheme, as better than none and in the hope that the Commissioners would come in time to see how inadequate it was. But the government was not so patient with Commissioners whom it considered to be governed by ignorance and egoism. It had before it the opinion of authorities such as the Army Sanitary Commission, which had written: "The town of Ahmedabad may be considered an extreme instance of sanitary neglect or indifference," and had urged "the absolute necessity of interference with the strong hand, either to compel the authorities to do their duty or to do it for them."[52] The government therefore declined to sanction expenditure on a project which it believed to be indefensible from both the sanitary and the economic points of view, and it ordered the Municipality to take the advice of experts. The press deplored this pressure, but it was effective. In 1888 the Municipal Commission agreed to put underground drainage in the Khadia ward, as an experiment. The experimental section

[51] *Ahmedabad Municipal Record*, no. 52, included in volume of Municipal *Proceedings* for 1898 (I).

[52] Memorandum, 4 Feb. 1887, Municipal *Compilation* of G.D. Resolutions Vol. IV (I).

was finished in 1895, and from 1903 onwards was extended to other parts of the city. Both the piped water-supply and the underground drainage were soon acknowledged to be boons to the city. Ranchhodlal was vindicated.

Ranchhodlal's service to his city brought praise in almost every official report on its administration. While he was President, the Ahmedabad Municipality was regarded by the government as the best example of local self-government in the Bombay Presidency outside the city of Bombay. It was far ahead of the others in public improvements. In 1894 the Collector, Mr. M. C. Gibb, wrote: "The Municipality is on the whole very well managed and the sanitary condition of the city would probably compare very favourably with many European cities."[53] But the improvements made during Ranchhodlal's time should not obscure the fact that Ripon's local self-government scheme was ultimately a failure in Ahmedabad. Without government support, Ranchhodlal would not have been able to succeed. The Western-educated politicians and elected representatives of the people were less progressive than either Ranchhodlal or the government. This experience of the character of the Ahmedabad and other mofussil municipalities, fulfilling their predictions at the time Ripon's schemes were introduced, contributed to the distrust government officers had of any extension of democratic institutions in India.

Ranchhodlal's improvements were costly and increased taxation was needed to meet the cost of servicing and repaying the loans which the city raised (at five per cent). Left to themselves the citizens of Ahmedabad, like those of other Indian cities, would have persisted with octroi and imposed tolls and duties on goods in transit—anything but a direct tax on themselves. The government was firmly opposed to octroi as a restraint on trade and even as a blot upon its administration. Just

[53] Collector to Commissioner, 2 Aug. 1894, Municipal *Report*, 1893–94 (II).

before it put pressure upon the Ahmedabad Municipality to accept the drainage scheme, it superseded the smaller Mehmadabad Municipality for continuing to levy octroi, and the Parantij Municipality was also superseded because it refused to introduce a house-tax. The Ahmedabad Municipality levied no house and property tax within the city walls, only in the unwalled suburbs inside municipal limits, where octroi could not be efficiently collected. One of the first acts of the elected Municipality in 1883 was to try to substitute octroi for the house-tax in the suburbs, but the government quashed this move. Other taxes were the income tax, the wheel tax, the toll on laden vehicles and animals entering the city, the halalkhore cess (for the cleaning of privies), and the tax for the collection of sullage water. Now there were the drainage tax and water-rate also. These taxes were bitterly criticized in the vernacular press.

In 1885 the Gujarat Sabha was formed for the purpose of representing "the wants of the people" to the government, a similar objective to that of the old Ahmedabad Association. Its secretary wrote a letter to the government about the constitution of the Municipal Commission, urging among other things that there should be special representation for the educated classes. It stated with reference to Lord Ripon's reforms: "It is principally to give scope to and take advantage of the legitimate ambition of this class that these administrative reforms are introduced, and it is therefore only proper that this class, which admittedly is in advance of the bulk of the population, should be recognised prominently."[54] In the next year a petition for political rights was presented to Lord Dufferin on behalf of the people of Ahmedabad, but not from the Municipality, and he refused to accept it.[55] Evidently Bechardas Ambaidas had much to do with this petition, which was inspired

[54] Letter to Bombay Government, 13 Jul. 1885, G.D. 95/1885 (I).
[55] Reports on Native Papers, Nov. 1886, J.D. 68D/1886 (I).

in part by ill-feeling towards Ranchhodlal. In 1888, a public
meeting presided over by Bechardas adopted a petition, signed
by 5,726 people, which pressed for reforms in local self-
government, including an elective two-thirds majority with
four representatives of the educated classes, and the right of
the Municipality to elect its own President. The government
conceded the right of the educated classes to elect two members (giving an elected majority) but denied the other requests
because it objected to the retention of octroi and the obstruction of Ranchhodlal's drainage and water-supply schemes. It
realized that he would no longer be President were the right
of election conceded to the commissioners.[56]

The vital role played by Ranchhodlal in the improvement
of the city was soon demonstrated by the decline which set in
after his death in 1898. In the next ten years there were four
different presidents. As early as 1902, successive Collectors began to complain of the inefficiency of the Municipality and the
"horrible and disgusting" condition of many parts of the city.
Encroachments and other violations of the municipal by-laws
were permitted, taxes were not properly collected, and the
municipal staff were lax and even corrupt. In 1909 the Commissioner of the Northern Division urged that the Municipality
be superseded for displaying an "almost criminal lack of business method," and apathy towards the city's sanitation and
water-supply incurring a serious danger of an outbreak of epidemic disease. In the disposal of land, public interests were
often being sacrificed to private. There was no lack of talk at
the meetings of the Municipal Commission; sometimes a single
point of order would take up a whole meeting. The Managing
and Sanitary Committees were in the hands of "the three most
obstructive members of the Municipality," Pherozshaw Kavasji and Ardeshir Kavasji (both Parsis), and Vankanthrai

[56] G.D. 82/1888 (I).

Ambalal, all of whom the President was too weak to control. As the Collector noted: "Ahmedabad is full of business men, but its Municipal affairs have come under the management of a singularly unbusinesslike body." This situation was brought about, he thought, by the ignorance of the voters, the failure of the more intelligent men to stand, and some corruption and gerrymandering. On 11 May 1910 the government reluctantly superseded the Ahmedabad Municipality for incompetence.[57] It was replaced by an appointed Committee of Management composed of able citizens and chaired by Sir Chinubhai Madhavlal, the grandson of Ranchhodlal. A Chief Officer from the government service had already been appointed in 1909. This appointed Committee worked well. Improved by-laws and rules were promulgated; the staff was reorganized; the water-supply and drainage systems were put into proper order and plans made for their further development; and a new terminal tax on goods coming within city limits replaced both the octroi within the city wall and the house-tax in the suburbs. In 1915, an elective Municipality was restored to the people of Ahmedabad, though the Chief Officer was replaced by a Municipal Commissioner with stronger powers.[58]

In the present century the Municipality has had to deal with many new problems. It had no sooner dealt with the modernization of the urban plant of the old city than it was faced with the problems brought by the great expansion of the cotton textile industry in Ahmedabad and its suburbs. The rapidly growing population intensified the problem of congestion within the walls and brought the need for amenities in the

[57] Collector (F. Pratt) to Commissioner, 3 Aug. 1902, G.D. 68/1902; G.D. 80/1909; 103/1910 (I).

[58] There were to be twenty-seven elected councillors and thirteen nominated, and the President was to be elected by a two-thirds majority of the councillors. Of the twenty-seven elected members, four were to be elected by the educated classes, one by the Millowners' Association, and twenty-two by wards.

suburbs. As early as 1872, the number of persons per square
mile within the Ahmedabad city wall was 53,435, greater than
in Bombay and double that in London. In the walled suburb of
Saraspur it was 63,914 per square mile, and in the more crowded quarters of the main city it was even greater. By 1902 the
density within the city limits was 60,000 per square mile and
in the Kalupur ward it was 120,000.[59] The southern and eastern wards of the city had been most densely populated at the
time the city came under British rule, but with the growth of
population and the greater security, most of the vacant ground
in the northern and western wards was built upon and it was
there that Ahmedabad's new courts, hospitals, churches, and
training college were built. There too her new residents, like
the Parsis, and, at first, the English officials, lived in detached
houses. Later, as the city filled up, the British moved nearer to
the cantonment to preserve their social distance.

The problems before the Municipality were not simply
due to the greater size and congestion of the city. The political,
social, and economic changes of the nineteenth century were
making for a different kind of urban environment. Among
them were the greater security, the weakening of the tight
control of caste and mahajan, and the formation of large industrial undertakings. One of the most important differences
between traditional and modern cities is, of course, the greater
differentiation of living and working quarters in the latter,
reaching its extreme in the contrast between the central city
area, deserted at night, and the dormitory suburbs of the modern Western city. This differentiation is to be found in modern
Ahmedabad, too, though to a lesser degree than in the typical
Western city. The suburbs of modern Ahmedabad are different in character from the puras of old Ahmedabad. They con-
tain bungalows inhabited by people who travel daily by bus

[59] Dr. Hewlett's report, G.D. 78/1875; G.D. 66/1903 (I).

or car to the city centre to work. Millowners, landed proprietors who lived in the city, and lawyers were among the first
to build bungalows. Some of these were within the city wall,
like the Parsi bungalows in Khanpur (in Shahpur ward), and
some were outside, especially in Shahibaug between the city
and the cantonment. Modern technology, in the shape of the
telephone in 1897, electricity in 1915, and the motor bus about
1921, also had an important influence on the spread of the
city, while tar sealing made the wider roads needed by modern
traffic tolerable in the dusty conditions of Ahmedabad.

At first the expansion of the city beyond the wall was not
haphazard. The memories of insecurity, and the occasional
experience of it still, persisted throughout most of the nineteenth century to make people reluctant to move far from protection, while there was also the social solidarity of caste to
influence residential patterns. The old custom for individuals
to found puras was revived, but most of these puras were for
warehouses to store goods outside of the range of the city's
octroi.[60] But in between the older practice of founding puras
and the twentieth century building societies and planned development had come a period of haphazard expansion of the city.
Mud and straw hovels proliferated wherever there was an
open space, within or without the walls. As Sardar Patel remarked in 1927: "Our cities are neither cities, nor villages.

[60] In 1847 Hathipura was founded by the merchant Hathising Kesrising; in 1879 it contained 62 warehouses and 40 inhabitants. In 1864
Fatehpura was founded by Fatesha, a Jain merchant; it had 15 warehouses and 44 servants and labourers. In 1865 Fulpura was founded
by Fulsha, a member of the Nagarseth family; in 1879 it had 27 buildings, mostly warehouses, and 67 people. These puras were for trading
rather than residential purposes. In 1871 the Collector founded Borradailepura for the use of the cultivators of the adjoining lands; in 1879
it had 61 houses and 170 people. In 1874 Uttampura was founded by
Uttamchand; it had 51 houses, and 170 inhabitants, chiefly day labourers. (*Ahmedabad Gazetteer*, p. 329) (II).

Many of our urban people live in rural conditions."[61] At first
the Municipality had thought of removing these people outside the city wall and a few were in fact resettled, but by 1890
it was listing as a municipal want the construction of chawls
for them. It did build some model chawls in 1899 but could not
afford to do more. Some of the millowners built chawls for
their workers outside the city walls. Within the wall, the squat-
ter problem was alleviated by the rising price of land. In 1883
the Collector, Mr. Richey, said that there were still large areas
within the city wall where the squatters could be concentrated,
but by 1905–6 it was noted: "The demand for land has of late
increased so much in the Municipal District that every vacant
spot of land which can be utilized for building a shop or house,
or put to any other profitable use, is greedily sought for by
them that invest their earnings in immoveable property."[62] The
mud and straw hovels were being pushed further out, beyond
the mills, and often beyond the municipal limits.

These limits were extended several times. The puras can
be represented on maps as small blocks, but as the city expanded with the growth of the mill industry and as security
improved, the suburbs became much more amorphous. Often
the same names were used for the older pura or village and
the newer industrial or residential suburb, which covered a
wider area. As a result, the areas which were included within
city limits did not correspond exactly with the older places
of the same name. In 1858 Hathipura, Madhavpura, and Rajpur
were included within municipal limits, but in 1860 were excluded when the limits were restricted to the area where
octroi could be efficiently collected—the main walled city and
the suburb Saraspur, which was also surrounded by a wall.
In 1875 part of the railway suburb was included. In 1879 the
Revenue Commissioner drew attention to the sanitary prob-

[61] Quoted in R. Parikh, p. 270 (III).
[62] Municipal *Reports*, 1889–90, and 1905–06 (II); Collector to Commissioner, 26 Feb. 1883, Municipal *Proceedings*, 10 Jul. 1883 (I).

lems caused by the exclusion of other suburbs and their consequent immunity from municipal control.[63] In 1881 the limits were extended to include Madhavpura, Hathipura, Borradailepura, Kangalpura, the rest of Railwaypura, and the tiny puras between these and the city. This took in the railway station and three mills. A house and property tax was levied there instead of octroi. In 1892 the Dudheshwar waterworks were included, and in 1900 Asarwa and the surrounding areas. In 1911 the Ellisbridge, Shahibaug and Gomtipur areas were included, and this brought the newer residential suburbs and more mills under the city's regulations and taxes.

The extensions brought petitions of protest from the people who lived in these areas. In 1875, 160 inhabitants of Railwaypura objected to their inclusion within the municipal limits, saying that the municipal commissioners lived in luxury, that the inspectors gave false information, and that they were disadvantaged because they had bought their land at high prices during the share mania.[64] It is easier to sympathise with the protest of the poor illiterate peasants of Asarwa, complaining that the first they knew their village had become part of the city of Ahmedabad was the serving of a property tax notice upon them. Again the government declined to interfere. Copies of the proclamation had been duly posted and no objections received.[65] In 1911 it was reported by the Collector, Mr. H. L. Painter, that the people of Asarwa village had been greatly harassed by the municipality's enforcement of its sanitary regulations, surely inappropriate for agriculturists, and that he had urged it to be less strict in such cases. In 1911 there were 119 petitions of protest about the extension of the municipal limits in that year.[66]

It was around the turn of the century that the first sug-

[63] N.D. Municipalities report, 1878–79 (G.D. 38/1879) (I).
[64] Petition of 26 Sep. 1875 (Boman-Behram, p. 418) (III).
[65] G.D. 69/1900 (I).
[66] G.D. 132/1911 (I).

gestions for planning the future expansion of the city were made. Until then government policy had not directed the city's development in a logical way but had created greater congestion. The street widening and the ruthless driving of main roads through the congested pols had simply compressed the caste communities still further. Large areas of land adjacent to the city were reserved by the British for their cantonment and civil lines, and Europeans lived there in bungalows set in spacious lots. The haphazard locations of the mills and their railway sidings prevented rational development to the east. To the west was the Sabarmati river. The present Ellis bridge was opened in 1892 to replace the one destroyed in the great flood of 1875. But there was no building on the western bank as late as 1902, though some land had been sold there at the time of the plague scare a few years before. The government had contributed to this situation through charging high prices for land outside the city and through selling land within the wall without restriction. But from 1897 the need to reserve land as an "air reservoir" or "lung" was recognised and sales were restricted. In 1899 the government handed over 16 acres of land to the municipality as "open-air spaces" to be kept for public use and planted with trees and shrubs. In 1901 the municipality asked the government to open up more agricultural land. The Collector reported at this time that there had been comparatively little building in the suburbs of Ahmedabad by persons other than millowners and admitted: "There may be some truth in the allegation that the rates prevailing hitherto have discouraged building and have only been possible for capitalist millowners who have had to build at any cost."[67] The government then reduced the rate of assessment. This encouraged building in the suburbs, and Ellisbridge soon

[67] Acting Collector (F. Pratt) to Commissioner, 12 Aug. 1902, R.D. resolution 7582, 28 Oct. 1902 (I).

began to develop as a residential area. A survey of the suburbs had been begun in 1896, and in 1901 the government urged the municipality to ensure they were developed in a planned way, with regard to the health and convenience of the people and avoiding the congestion of the old city. In 1910 the government gave the city 50,000 rupees to further the work of city improvement. In 1916, following the Bombay Town Planning Act of 1915, a comprehensive plan was prepared by Mr. A. E. Mirams, Consulting Surveyor to the Government of Bombay.[68]

One of the most controversial issues was the city wall which had figured so prominently in the early history of municipal government in Ahmedabad. In 1875 Dr. Hewlett suggested that it be pulled down to improve ventilation but Mr. Borradaile objected, saying that the people would be opposed and that it was a safeguard against the city being swept away in floods, such as the recent one in which it had in fact been a useful barrier. In 1888 the Collector, Mr. H. E. M. James, said that the removal of the wall would permit the expansion of the city towards the railway station and that few but antiquarians would object. In 1894 the Sanitary Commissioner urged it also, but the Municipality resolved that it would be inadvisable. In 1911 the police proposed to remove part of the wall and to fill up the space with police lines. The government then began to give serious consideration to demolishing the wall in order to give more light and air to the city, improve access to the suburbs, and create a "ringstrasse" around the city. A government committee reported in favour of this in 1915. At this point, Professor Patrick Geddes, the noted British town planning authority, who had been invited by the Government of Madras to enlighten the municipal authorities and public on the subject of modern town planning, was en-

[68] G.D. 72/1901; G.D. comp. 658/1916 (I).

gaged by the Government of Bombay to give his advice on the problems of a number of cities in the Bombay Presidency.[69]

Patrick Geddes wrote a number of reports in India, including one in which he opposed the removal of Ahmedabad's wall. On the whole his reports did not please the Bombay Government, which, while acknowledging that they had inspired local bodies with a desire for urban improvements, thought that "the value of his teaching was impaired by the strong element of vague idealism which pervaded it, by lack of familiarity with local conditions and requirements, by a tendency to evade recognition of the practical difficulties which have to be faced in dealing with the question of town planning in India, and by a general avoidance of points relating to the technique of town planning. They were for the most part deficient in useful practical suggestions." But Geddes's report on Ahmedabad reflected the great respect for tradition, for history, and for local customs, which was a hallmark of his approach to town planning and which had hitherto been lacking in the improvements carried out in that city and elsewhere in India. Instead of the ruthless driving of wide straight roads through the crowded quarters of India's cities— which, as we have seen in the case of Ahmedabad, made urban congestion worse, not better—Geddes favoured the method of "conservative surgery," by which the local environment was carefully studied, and only certain buildings removed. No one has written in more glowing terms of Ahmedabad than Geddes: of her old architecture, her pols, her Kankaria, and her historic wall.[70] But his advice to retain the city wall was not followed, except for a small part which still remains.

[69] G.D. 78/1875; 97/1876; 13/1889; G.D. comps. 869/1915, 896/1915. Municipal *Proceedings*, 29 May, 1894 (I).

[70] G.D. comps. 752/1915; 896/1915 (contains Geddes's report on the Ahmedabad wall); 1121/1915; 1005/1916 (I); see Tyrwhitt (ed.), *Patrick Geddes in India* (III).

Although the physical environment of Ahmedabad had been much improved by the time of the First World War, conditions were still far from perfect. The death-rate, particularly of children, remained high until well into the twentieth century, when it became clear that the problem was not as simple as Ranchhodlal and Colonel Ducat had believed.[71] There was less cholera but the water-supply scheme, which provided abundant water before there was adequate underground drainage, led to an increase in malaria as the hollows in and around the city filled with water and became breeding places for the anopheles mosquito. In 1916 the mortality was still 39.22 per thousand (double that of Surat) and doctors disagreed about the causes: malaria, or the insanitary and muddy state of the pols.[72] The millowners did not bother to seal the ground around their mills which was covered with pools of waste water. To the dust that had always plagued Ahmedabad were added smoke and soot. The Municipality did maintain the gardens in the Karanj and at Kankaria. Ranchhodlal put a fountain in the Karanj at his own expense, and in 1902 the Victoria Memorial Gardens were started. But so far there were few amenities that were not starkly utilitarian—and this reflected Ahmedabad's priorities.

This has been the story of the transformation of an old city into a modern one. It has not been "a tale of two cities," not the history of the creation of a new Western city side by side with a traditional city, as in the case of Cairo or Delhi. The first textile mills were within the wall, the next just outside the gates. It was in the old city that modern street lighting, road sealing, drainage, and water were first provided, and it

[71] Infant mortality, 1893–97: Ahmedabad city 358 per thousand; Ahmedabad district rural areas, 176 per thousand (G.D. 66/1903) (I).

[72] Annual report Bechardas dispensary, 1894 (Municipal *Compilation*, Slaughter-houses) (I); Collector to Commissioner, 1 Jul. 1892 (Municipal *Report*, 1893–94) (II); G.D. 66/1903; 658/1916 (I).

was there that the controversy over the improvements took place. Ranchhodlal, the originator both of Ahmedabad's textile industry and of her modern drainage and water-supply, was himself an Ahmedabadi. The transformation of the elite of the old city has gone hand in hand with the incoming of people from the towns and villages of Gujarat. In the twentieth century Ahmedabad has expanded far beyond the area formerly enclosed within the wall, and the spacious, planned suburbs provide a new type of life, but they were first inhabited by people whose families already had houses in the old city, and characteristically, they were planned as cooperative enterprises, like the pols of the old city. Ahmedabad remains true to its past, a city of orthogenetic change.[73]

[73] Cf. Redfield and Singer, "The Cultural Role of Cities" (III).

CHAPTER V

Beyond the Wall

As in other parts of India, the final two years of the First World War and the early years of the peace were a watershed in the history of Ahmedabad. The city emerged from the war economically stronger than ever and the last fifty years have seen more social, political, and even visual change than the preceding century. Before the war, Ahmedabad was an unknown, parochial place lightly ruled by the British. After the war it became, in fact if not in law, a financial and political base for the Indian National Congress and a leader and prototype of New India. Ahmedabad became the home of Mahatma Gandhi and Sardar Patel, and there they acquired much of their political experience.

The war was a boon to the Ahmedabad textile industry because it stopped the imports from Lancashire. Ahmedabad

had no export trade outside India to lose and it was now able
to extend its strong hold over the local market in coarse fabrics
to medium price *dhoties*, *saries* and shirtings. Great profits
were earned but, in contrast to Bombay, over-capitalization
was avoided. As Kasturbhai Lalbhai has written:

> Even though the people found that over-night they were
> able to secure incomes, which could not have entered their
> wildest imagination earlier, true to their traditional make-up,
> they did not lose their grip on the essentially temporary
> character of the phenomenon. While their standard of liv-
> ing did not remain entirely unaffected, much the major part
> of what they earned they saved, with the result that after the
> frenzied period was over, not only were the people them-
> selves moderately rich, but the mill companies also could
> show enviable reserves. Again, on account of the hereditary
> element in the Industry, the higher earning power or the
> larger reserves were not cashed by over-capitalization, and
> in the face of overwhelming temptation, scarcely any mill
> changed hands. In this way, the War converted the mills and
> the agents into powerful industrialists. Still, in keeping with
> traditional policy, this success was achieved so quietly that
> even competent observers failed to notice that Ahmedabad
> was destined to play a very important role in the near future.[1]

The inter-war years were not a period of prosperity for
Indian industry in general, but Ahmedabad managed better
than many industrial centres. The Ahmedabad mills prospered
at times when the Bombay mills were unable to pay dividends
at all. Lower overheads, dedicated, economical and personal
management, and cheaper and more settled labour were important reasons. The Ahmedabad mills were also showing
themselves to be more adaptable in adopting new methods

[1] Rotary Club of Ahmedabad, p. 35 (III).

and switching to the production of the high counts. Sir Chinubhai Madhavlal was the first to attempt to produce the high counts from Egyptian cotton, but in the 1920's the Calico Mill set the pace. The Ahmedabad textile industry now produces finer cloth than most of the other Indian mill centres. Other important factors in Ahmedabad's inter-war prosperity were protection, *swadeshi*, and good labour relations.

During and after the war, as India acquired more fiscal autonomy, the rates of duty on imported textiles were steadily increased, especially to meet the growing competition from Japan. The Ahmedabadi millowner, Kasturbhai Lalbhai, led the fight in the Indian Legislative Assembly for the abolition of the cotton excise which had first been imposed in 1896 as a countervailing duty on Indian domestic textile production equivalent to the duty on imported cotton piece goods. After a major debate in 1924 the Government of India suspended the excise in 1925 and abolished it in 1926. The swadeshi movement for the purchase of Indian-made articles in preference to imported goods, which followed the agitation over the partition of Bengal in 1905, was intensified by Mahatma Gandhi in 1930. The Ahmedabad mills, with their reserves, their carefully maintained and regularly replaced modern machinery, and their wide market organization, were ready to take advantage of both protection and swadeshi and contributed to the success of both.

The Ahmedabad mills have also enjoyed better labour relations than other Indian textile centres, notably Bombay. Apart from occasional stoppages for a day or so, because of dissatisfaction over fining for absence or bad work or over attempted reductions in wages, major strikes were unknown in the city until 1895. In that year 8,000 mill workers carried out an unsuccessful and violent strike for eight days, in protest against the decision of the Ahmedabad Millowners' Association (formed in 1891) that wages be paid fortnightly instead of weekly.[2] In subsequent years there were strikes in individual mills, generally over wages, but no serious trouble until the later years of the First World War.

Just before the war Miss Anasuyabehn Sarabhai, the sister of the millowner Ambalal Sarabhai, returned from Europe deeply impressed by new ideals of social service. She decided to devote her time to education and social reform among the workers of Ahmedabad. She collected a small band of helpers and started a night school in a working class area in 1916. Late in 1917 there was a strike of warpers in the Ahmedabad mills, after warpers from Bombay and other places were engaged through the Millowners' Association. For some time the warpers had been pressing for an increase in their wages. Like others in Ahmedabad they were feeling the growing gap between wartime prices and wages. Anasuyabehn organised the workers and a settlement of the strike was reached after a fortnight. The modern trade union movement of Ahmedabad dates its foundation from this event. In February 1918 there was to be a more important dispute in which Mahatma Gandhi became involved.

Not long after his return from South Africa Gandhi came to live in Ahmedabad. He founded his Satyagraha Ashram there on 25 May 1915 in Kochrab village, and he later moved it to Sabarmati. It was from there that he left in 1930 to lead the Salt March, which initiated the second great round of national Satyagraha (non-violent resistance). In his *Autobiography* he wrote:

> I had a predilection for Ahmedabad. Being a Gujarati I thought I should be able to render the greatest service to the country through the Gujarati language. And then, as Ah-

[2] Bombay Government, *Provincial Report on the Working of the Indian Factories Act, 1895* (II).

medabad was an ancient centre of handloom weaving, it was likely to be the most favourable field for the revival of the cottage industry of hand-spinning. There was also the hope that, the city being the capital of Gujarat, monetary help from its wealthy citizens would be more available here than elsewhere.[3]

The origins of Mahatma Gandhi's ideas, and particularly the characteristic Gujarati element in them, have not been fully explored by scholars. Ahimsa, the hartal, communal tolerance and peaceful settlement of disputes, frugality and self-reliance, acceptance both of capital and of the dignity of labour, and respect for women, were typically, if not uniquely Gujarati. The Gujaratis recognized the new commercial and industrial society for what it was, the dangers as well as the opportunities, and Gandhi, who promoted hand spinning, and the millionaire industrialists of Ahmedabad were firm friends. It was not only because both he and they were Gujaratis that Gandhi found a congenial home among the Ahmedabadis and a place in their hearts unrivalled elsewhere in India; it was also because Ahmedabad was a city which had not lost its corporate identity and been swept overboard by the West but which valued traditional culture, social responsibility, and harmony.

Nowhere in India was Gandhi more looked up to for guidance on matters of the day than he was in Ahmedabad. He soon became involved in the problems of labour. Since 1916 the millowners had been paying a bonus in order to keep their labour force during a plague epidemic, and in some cases this had reached as much as 70 per cent of the wage. Early in 1918 they decided to replace it by an increase of wages of only 20 per cent, but prices had risen considerably since 1916, and the weavers asked for an increase of 50 per cent. Serious

[3] M. K. Gandhi, *The Story of My Experiments with Truth*, p. 291 (III).

trouble was in the offing, and both sides asked Gandhi to intervene. An arbitration board was set up, but before it could begin its work, there was a hasty strike by workers in a few mills. The employers reacted with a lock-out, all the mills were closed, and 10,000 weavers were out for four weeks. The millowners and government officers were afraid that there would be violence. Gandhi and Anasuyabehn addressed the workers daily in the riverbed and urged them to stand firm on a demand for a 35 per cent increase, and remain non-violent. After a month, when it seemed that the millowners would win, Gandhi, stung (so it was said) by taunts that he was well fed though the workers were starving, resolved to fast until they received what they were asking for. The millowners capitulated, afraid that if Gandhi died the workers would wreak vengeance on them and on their mills. A face-saving formula that an arbitrator would be appointed was followed by the granting of the 35 per cent increase. Gandhi and Anasuyabehn were revered by the mill workers as their benefactors. During the struggle the workers became well-organized and accustomed to meetings, to common counsel, and to concerted action.[4]

In 1920 the Ahmedabad Textile Labour Association, or Majur Mahajan, was formed to carry on labour work on Gandhian lines. Gandhi guided its work for many years. He was a member of the permanent Board of Arbitration on behalf of the workers until 1935, and a member of the Advisory Committee until his death. The Majur Mahajan has been from its foundation one of the best organized and best conducted trade unions in India. It emphasizes peaceful industrial relations, class cooperation, arbitration, and social service among its members. On the whole it has been successful in containing

[4] On this dispute, see Disorders Inquiry Committee, *Evidence*, Vol. II (II); M. H. Desai, *A Righteous Struggle*; I. K. Yajnik, *Gandhi as I Know Him* (III).

industrial trouble—too successful according to Gandhi's left-wing critics, such as his old fellow-worker Indulal Yajnik. There have been no major non-political strikes in Ahmedabad since 1923. In that year the employers proposed a cut in wages because of the depressed state of the textile industry. After a strike lasting 10 weeks the workers were forced to give in, and an arbitrator's award led to a cut in wages of 15½ per cent. Gandhi regarded the Majur Mahajan as a model to be followed elsewhere in India but, as the Royal Commission on Labour in India noted in 1931, its success in Ahmedabad depended very largely on unique circumstances. The employers and employees were alike Gujaratis, and Mahatma Gandhi enjoyed such prestige in the city that both had immense confidence in his sense of fairness and sympathy towards them. They would have been faced with serious difficulties if they had opposed his views.[5] It could be added that the Majur Mahajan has carried on the traditions of the mahajans of old Ahmedabad, and it is not in the least remarkable to anyone familiar with the history of that city and of Gujarat that she should have evolved a unique and highly successful system of industrial arbitration and that she should have nurtured Mahatma Gandhi.

In the twentieth century, the millowners and other people of Ahmedabad began to take an interest in wider national questions affecting their interests. Earlier, a few prominent Ahmedabad citizens, including Nagarseth Premabhai Hemabhai and Bechardas Ambaidas, had served on the Bombay Legislative Council. In 1893 the Bombay Provincial Conference was held in Ahmedabad. But modern political activity was slow to develop in Ahmedabad compared to Bengal or Maharashtra, though there was, as we have seen, no lack of enterprise in other directions. Modern politics first developed within the new legal profession, which was to a large extent composed

[5] Karnik, pp. 91–107 (III).

of newcomers to the city. The formation of the Ahmedabad
Association and Gujarat Sabha has already been noted in connection with municipal affairs. The leading members of the
Gujarat Sabha were pleaders, and significantly, its first secretary, Mr. M. P. Modi, was a Parsi. A later secretary and chief
organizer was another outsider, the pleader Govindrao Apaji
Patil, a Maharashtrian Brahmin. The Sabha published a
monthly paper for a while; it started night classes for labourers,
a Gokhale Society, and the Dadabhai Naoroji Library.[6] The
Gujarat Sabha was not a militant body until it was revitalized
by Mahatma Gandhi in 1917. After 1920 it was absorbed into
the Indian National Congress and became the Gujarat Provincial Congress Committee.

In 1902 the Indian National Congress held its annual session in Ahmedabad. The president of the reception committee
was Ambalal Sakerlal Desai. He was a Brahma-Kshatriya who,
after retirement from the service of Baroda State, where he
had risen to be Chief Justice of the Supreme Court, started
three textile mills. His motives were patriotic in part. However,
he was unsuccessful in business. In his address of welcome he
referred to Ahmedabad's new realization of the importance
of politics, brought about by such issues as: the cotton excise
of 1896, which had led to the stopping of several mills in Ahmedabad, the currency legislation, the collection of land revenue during the recent famine, and the treatment of Indians
in South Africa. The local delegates to the Congress included
the Nagarseth and the leading millowners of the city.[7] One
of the first Congress organisers in Ahmedabad was Shivabhai
Motibhai Patel, who came to Ahmedabad from Kaira in 1894
and was one of the first of many Lewa Patidars from that district to become important in the city.

The rise and diffusion of the Patidars of Kaira is one of

[6] Shankerlal Amritray, pp. 103–104 (III).
[7] *Report of the Eighteenth Indian National Congress* (III).

the most significant stories in the modern social history of
Gujarat. From about the time of the First World War this
community has played an important role in the economic and
political life of Ahmedabad. Kaira (Kheda) was the richest
and most densely populated district of the old Bombay Presidency, probably the richest in India per capita. She had fertile
soil, a long-existing market for her food grains in Ahmedabad
and neighboring towns, and above all, a tough, independent,
and enterprising class of peasant proprietors, the Lewa Patidars.
These comprised a number of lineages of Gujar stock and
Kanbi caste which had settled between the Sabarmati and
Mahi rivers and established an ascendancy over the local tribes
of Kolis and Bhils. Under the Muslim and Maratha rulers, they
competed for power with Koli, Rajput, and Muslim lineages.
Patidar originally referred to the "shareholders"—those among
the Kanbis who were jointly responsible for the payment of
the land revenue of the village—but in the twentieth century,
the name Patidar was applied to the whole caste and the original
distinction was blurred.

Under the British the Patidars of Kaira district were able
to maintain their position as the dominant lineages in the area.
They were de facto rulers of their villages. Their hold was
fortified by the revenue settlements, which were made to them
as groups and not, as was normally the case elsewhere in the
Bombay Presidency, with taluqdars or with individual peasant
proprietors. The Maratha system of farming the revenues had
disorganized village life elsewhere but the Patidars had been
strong enough to deal with the Marathas as groups and keep
control of their villages. The British found it convenient to
keep this practice. In addition, they aimed to create in Gujarat
a class of substantial independent cultivators with capital for
agricultural improvement and largely freed from the surveil-
lance of government officers. In this they were successful.
The rest of the nineteenth century saw the Patidars consoli-

date their position relative to the Rajputs, Muslims, and Kolis through the extension of the cash economy, money-lending, education, and posts in the revenue administration. Men who could read and write were preferred for the post of village manager, and this made the Patidars anxious to teach their sons.

During most of the nineteenth century, rural Gujarat was prosperous in relation to its past and to most other parts of India. Peace and order, a great extension of the production of cash crops—notably cotton, tobacco and food grains—and the development of communications brought wealth to the Patidars. Much of this was invested in agricultural improvements and in building up the best cattle stocks in the whole of India. The competition from imported and locally made machine produced textiles brought distress to the low caste weavers, and increasing pressure on the land forced an increasing proportion of the Dharalas into agricultural labour for others. But the Vanias and Patidars throve on the new opportunities brought by the Pax Britannica and money economy. However, from the end of the century this prosperity was arrested in rural Gujarat, particularly in Kaira. In 1899 the monsoon failed and famine came to Gujarat for two years, for the first time since 1812. Government and people alike were ill prepared because almost everyone had come to believe that the area was immune to famine. The government lacked experience in handling relief works and revenue remissions. The people no longer kept their old stores of food grains but sent their surplus off to market, and they lacked (so the government officers said) the hardiness of the Deccanis, who were used to scarcity and famine. Kaira was the worst affected district. The deaths were almost entirely confined to the lower classes of the population, and among them the youngest and oldest were worst hit. To the Patidars, the loss of most of their cattle was more important, because in rural Gujarat, even more than in other areas, wealth was invested in cattle.

Further misfortunes followed. In 1901 huge tracts of Kaira district were devastated by locusts and in 1902 overrun by rats, thereby converting a moderate scarcity into another year of intense distress. The Bombay Government was not generous in the remission of land revenue, and there was much disappointment among the Patidars, who noted that the government had spent money keeping alive the classes beneath them. From 1901 to 1910, there was greater mortality from plague in Kaira than in any other district of Gujarat. After the famine, Kaira largely switched from wet to dry cultivation, from rice to *bajri* and cotton. The famine and other calamities stimulated emigration from Kaira district of the upwardly-mobile Patidars. Already increasing numbers of the Patidars had been taking to trade as, with the increasing population, many of them had found it hard to obtain a sufficiently large share of land. In Baroda State, free and compulsory primary education had been introduced in a small area in 1893, and in the next 13 years had been nominally extended to the whole State. This also provided a stimulus to emigration. Patidars went to Bombay, to East Africa, and to other places throughout the world. Many went to the city of Ahmedabad, and a large number of these found employment in the mills as technical and administrative staff; some eventually became mill-owners. Generally the Patidars comprise much of the middle class of modern Ahmedabad. This new elite was more politically conscious than the Vania elite of the old city.[8]

Serious political organization and activity, which was affiliated to action in the rest of India, first came to Ahmedabad and Kaira with the formation of a branch of the Home Rule

[8] On the Patidars and famine, see Indian Famine Commission, 1901, *Evidence*; *Census Reports*, Vol. IX (1901) and Vol. VII pt. I (1911) (II); A. M. Shah, "Political System in Eighteenth Century Gujarat" (III); *Gazetteer, Kaira and Panch Mahals* (II); Pocock "The Movement of Castes"; Nair, pp. 170–178 (III).

League in Ahmedabad on 6 October 1916 by two local bar-
risters, Maganbhai Chaturbhai Patel and Jivanlal Varajrai
Desai. They were aided by the Gokhale Society and the
Swadeshi Mitra Mandal. In that year, the Bombay Provincial
Conference and the Gujarat Educational Conference had
aroused some interest in the city, and in the previous year the
Bombay Congress also. Most of the members of the Home Rule
League were Brahma-Kshatriyas. A meeting, held under the
chairmanship of Mahatma Gandhi and addressed by Mr. P. K.
Telang from Bombay, was attended by about 1000 people,
chiefly students and members of the legal profession. The
League was given more impetus by the internment of Mrs.
Annie Besant by the Madras Government in June 1917, and a
deputation from Bombay came to Ahmedabad, spoke at a public meeting, and injected more life into the local branch. Open-
air street lectures were begun. The League began sending delegates to the country districts, and on 1 July 1917, a branch was
opened at Nadiad, the chief town of the Kaira district, which
by now was very closely tied to Ahmedabad in various ways.
Within a short time, eighty-six active branches were at work
in Kaira district distributing Home Rule literature and col-
lecting signatures for the Home Rule petition to be forwarded
to the Secretary of State for India. In August, the Ahmedabad
branch held a meeting for which special invitations had been
issued to the trading class. Following this meeting, fifty traders
were enrolled. This broadened political activity beyond the
Western-educated professional people to whom it had been
confined previously.

The extension of political activity in Ahmedabad and
Kaira was closely linked to the association of Mahatma Gandhi
and the Home Rule League with the redress of local and popular grievances. If the Home Rule League had not devoted
attention to these local problems, it could not have garnered

such a broad base of support from the Ahmedabadis, since purely national issues would have had little real meaning. The war had brought a great rise in the prices of essential commodities, shortages, and rationing with the inevitable clumsiness, petty corruption, and irritations involved in its administration. The activities of recruiters and collectors of war loans had also aroused resentment. The government was held responsible for the behaviour of its subordinate officers and any extension of government activities was resented by a community whose traditional attitude to government had been to keep out of its way. This was even more true when the government was represented on the spot by a not infrequently corrupt petty-fogging official, tax-gatherer, or policeman, anxious to curry favour with his English superiors by zealous prosecution of the war effort, far from the battlefields of Europe or Mesopotamia. The agitation against the Rowlatt Bills begun by Mahatma Gandhi in 1919 owed much of its success to a widespread impression that the police were to be given added power to harass anyone they liked, including respectable people. The scarcity of food and the influenza pandemic of 1918–19 also added to popular discontent, for which the government provided an obvious target. Gandhi's association with the textile labourers' strike had been particularly important in increasing respect for him in Ahmedabad.

The campaign he led against the payment of land revenue in Kaira had similar effects. Excessive monsoon rains had damaged the crops in that district in the revenue year 1917–18 and, as in the great famine, the government's remissions of land revenue were considered to be insufficient by the farmers. The Home Rule League started an agitation. Gandhi became the leader and took the view that it was the duty of all to refuse to pay the land revenue. Sacred vows not to pay were collected by the local branch of the Home Rule League. Eventually a compromise was arrived at under which the well-to-do paid up, and the revenue of the rest was suspended; this seems to have been regarded as a victory by both sides. Gandhi and the Home Rule League were regarded as benefactors by the peasantry of Kaira who acquired a new consciousness of politics and of their collective strength. The work done by the League in providing relief during the influenza pandemic and famine gave it added prestige.

On 23 February 1919 a public meeting was held in Ahmedabad to protest against the Rowlatt Bills. It was presided over by Vallabhbhai Patel, a Lewa Patidar from Kaira district who had come to Ahmedabad as a lawyer and had become converted to Gandhi's variety of nationalism. On the following day another meeting was held at Gandhi's ashram which was attended by leading nationalists from Bombay, and there it was decided to start a passive resistance campaign unless the Rowlatt Bills were dropped. The *Satyagraha* manifesto and vow, to refuse civilly to obey the Rowlatt laws and other laws to be designated by a committee to be appointed, were published. Posters with quotations from Thoreau on civil disobedience appeared and there were meetings of protest about the Rowlatt Bills. The Satyagraha Sabha was formed on 20 March and the Home Rule League was merged with it. The Rowlatt Act was passed on 18 March and received the Viceroy's sanction on 21 March. Meetings in Ahmedabad, Nadiad, and other places in Gujarat were addressed by Sarojini Naidu, the poetess, and by Swami Shraddhanand from Delhi, who gave the Satyagraha movement a religious significance. Ten thousand mill hands attended a meeting he addressed in Ahmedabad on 20 March, the anniversary of the settlement of the textile strike. The news of the disorder in Delhi on 30 March added to the excitement in the city. On 6 April Ahmedabad observed a day of national penance and mourning, of fast and prayer.

The largest crowd yet seen in the city (between 50,000 and 100,000 people) took out a procession and assembled to hear speeches. All sections of the community were represented and there was a general hartal. As yet, however, there was no violence.

The people of Ahmedabad could hardly be described as "turbulent" or "prone to violence," quite the contrary. But on the evening of 8 April 1919 the Bombay Government ordered Mahatma Gandhi to get down from the train on his way to the Punjab and on 10 April the report reached Ahmedabad that he had been arrested. The mill hands stopped work, shops closed, and excited crowds gathered in the streets shouting "Mahatma Gandhi ki Jai" (Victory to Mahatma Gandhi). People were ordered to get down from vehicles and proceed on foot. When two Europeans resisted, they were attacked and in the process an Indian policeman was killed. On the morning of the 11th the people were further incensed by a false rumour that Anasuyabehn had been arrested too. Crowds up to a thousand strong, and apparently composed of mill workers in the main, equipped with kerosene and syringes and armed with sticks and agricultural implements, proceeded to burn down the Collector's office and other government buildings in the city, including a large number of police posts. A European Sergeant of Police was killed and the houses of two Indian officials were wrecked. At least twenty-eight people were killed and one hundred twenty-three wounded in firing by the police and military. On the next day, there were disturbances at Viramgam, telegraph wires were cut at several places in Kaira district; and a troop train was derailed on its way to Ahmedabad. By the fourteenth, complete order had been restored and things returned to normal very quickly. This was attributed by the Collector of Ahmedabad to the fact that the motive for the rioting had been largely personal affection for Gandhi and that when his safety was assured, all reason for it ceased. But other important factors were the presence of troops and the fact that the crowd had already made its point by destroying the major part of the government's property within the city.

The disturbances of April 1919 marked the transfer of moral authority in Ahmedabad from the British Government to the Indian National Congress. The government proceeded to punish the city by making a financial levy on all mill workers, income tax payers, and houseowners. This reflected its belief that the responsibility for the riots extended beyond the ranks of those involved. There can be little doubt that the feelings of the rioters about the rumoured arrest of Gandhiji were shared by many respectable people, who would have shrunk from violence themselves. They did little to assist the government in the subsequent investigations and prosecutions in Ahmedabad which resulted in the conviction of one hundred six people—only a fraction of those involved. Much of the evidence presented before a special tribunal in Ahmedabad and before another which tried the cases in Kaira district, and before the subsequent Disorders Inquiry Committee—the Hunter Committee—was of a very impressionistic kind. Several of the local British officials believed that the riots had been organized beforehand, and curiously this view was shared by Mahatma Gandhi, who made the statement that educated people were involved. However, other Satyagraha workers, including Indulal Yajnik, who were actually on the spot, were firm that Gandhi was mistaken in this view. It is possible that there was some ad hoc organization on the night of the 10th or morning of the 11th, if only by leaders among the mill workers, but at this point analysis must give way to speculation. As Indulal Yajnik wrote afterwards, "the conscious leaders and workers who had been carrying on propaganda till the morning of 10th April had not only no hand in the riots, but [that] all of them were thoroughly dumbfound on seeing the burning lava of popular fury that began, as it were, to suddenly spout forth with demonical energy from some mysterious subterranean vaults and that kindled hell-fires all over the city for three mad days."[9] To Mahatma Gandhi and his fellow workers, the riots in Ahmedabad and elsewhere showed the need for very great caution in stirring up the masses and for education in the principles of Satyagraha. To the people of Gujarat and the rest of India and to the government, they showed that the Mahatma was now unquestionably the leading political figure of post-war India. In Ahmedabad and Kaira the Congress went from strength to strength.[10]

From that time onwards, the history of the Ahmedabad Municipality was bound up with the Indian national movement. In 1917 Sardar Vallabhbhai Patel, who was to become the most famous of all the Lewa Patidars, had been elected to the Municipal Commission. He was particularly active in criticizing the high-handedness of the British Municipal Commissioner, incompetence in the water-supply, and evasion of taxes. He built up a party within the Commission and after the election of 1919 his supporters increased in number. In 1920 the Municipality won the right to select its own Municipal Commissioner, though at first he had to be from the government service, and an Indian was appointed. From this time onwards there was a disengagement of Europeans from the Municipality's service. In February 1921, in compliance with Gandhi's call for a boycott of government educational institutions, the Ahmedabad Municipality resolved to embark on non-

[9] Yajnik, pp. 97–98 (III).

[10] This account of the disturbances of 1919 is largely based on Disorders Inquiry Committee, *Evidence*, Vol. II (II); *Proceedings*, Government of India, Home Department (Political), 192–198, July 1919; 451–452A, Sep. 1919; 309B, Oct. 1919; 399–410B, Jan. 1920 (I). I am presently preparing a more detailed paper on this subject.

cooperation with the government in educational matters, and
declined to accept either the government's grant or its right to
inspect the municipal schools. As a result it was superseded by
the government in 1922. Ramanbhai Mahipatram Nilkanth, the
son of Mahipatram Rupram, had been the very able President
of the Municipality since 1916 and, because he was one of the
"moderates," who did not support non-cooperation, he continued as Chairman of the Committee of Management after the
supersession.

In 1924 the Municipality was reinstated, elections were
held, and Sardar Patel became President. He carried through
a vigorous programme of improvement, in accordance with
his view that: "The test of municipal improvement is how it
works in the poor localities."[11] During his term as President,
the Municipality extended the water-supply and drainage,
planned gardens, parks, and playing fields for schools, and
initiated the Kankaria and Ellisbridge planning schemes (under
which these areas developed as planned suburbs, in conjunction
with the cooperative housing societies), the Kalupur relief road
(now called Tilak road) and the removal of the city wall.
(These last two aroused strong opposition: the first because
of the division of the pols and the compulsory acquisitions, the
second for reasons of sentiment and imagined security). In
1928 Sardar Patel resigned after losing his majority to a group
led by Ambalal Sarabhai. There had been friction between the
Municipality and the millowners, chiefly over increases in the
water-rates paid by industrial establishments and the provision
of services to the mill areas.[12] But the opposition to Vallabhbhai
was (it is said in Ahmedabad) entirely personal: he was a
tough, high-handed administrator, as he demonstrated later on
the national stage.

But Ahmedabad soon became involved in the national

[11] Quoted in R. Parikh, p. 271. On Sardar Patel's work in Ahmedabad, see N. D. Parikh, *Sardar Vallabhbhai Patel*, Vol. I (III).
[12] Ahmedabad Millowners' Association, *Report*, 1928–29, p. 9 (III).

struggle which was resumed by Mahatma Gandhi in 1930. The Hindu and Jain professional and commercial people and mill-owners provided strong support for the Congress. In 1931 the Municipality refused to cooperate in the decennial national census. But the government took no action against it until 23 September 1942 when it was superseded, this time for en-dorsing the All-India Congress Committee's "Quit India" reso-lution. At this time the textile workers were on strike and the mills had to close. The government handed over the city's administration to government officers and imprisoned several municipal officers, who had also been on strike. In 1944 an election was held, but the Congress won and the newly elected Municipality declared the previous supersession illegal. On 13 April 1944 the Municipality was again superseded and replaced by a Board of Management until 1946. The citizens of Ah-medabad are rightly proud of the part they played in the Indian independence movement.[13]

The most tragic problem of modern Indian political his-tory—the communal problem—has fortunately played only a small role in the history of Ahmedabad. This accords with the spirit of sensible compromise and tolerance evident in other aspects of Ahmedabadi life, such as the mahajan tradition and the good relations between capital and labour. This is not to say, however, that there has never been any communal trouble in Ahmedabad. In 1714 there was rioting at the time of the Holi celebrations.[14] The political rivalries between Mughal and Maratha officers for power in the city, and commercial rivalries between Hindu and Bohora merchants, were also reflected in religious tensions, though they were to some extent reflections of that tension. There were no recorded riots between the two communities for two centuries.

One cause of friction was the butchering of animals by

[13] Mavalankar and Dalal, *Rashtriya Chalvalman Amdavad Munici-palityno Falo* (III).

[14] Ali Muhammed Khan, *Mirat-i-Ahmadi*, pp. 358–359 (III).

Muslims. A principle which is very dear to the Hindu and Jain population of Ahmedabad is the sanctity of all life; the panjarapol is one of the main charities of the city. Stray or dangerous animals were removed from the city rather than killed. In 1896 the Municipality resolved not to contribute towards the killing of stray dogs, so as not to hurt the feelings of the mahajans who spent a good sum in removing them from the city. In 1899 there were riots in the city when an Englishman opened a slaughter-house, with the intention of exporting hides to the leather industry at Kanpur. In 1911 there was a general hartal in protest against the police poisoning stray dogs. The shops remained closed for several days. The Municipality repeatedly deferred the opening of a municipal slaughter-house and meat and fish markets, though it was long recognised that the unhygienic conditions under which the Muslim butchers worked were most dangerous to the health of the community. The Municipality did, however, makes rules about where the butchers could kill animals. They were compelled to put up a slaughter-house for cattle instead of killing them on their own premises. The butchers put up petitions of protest about the expense of this, but there were also protests from Hindus and Jains about the proximity of the slaughter-houses to their homes and about animals being led through the streets to execution. Sometimes Hindu policemen would take it upon themselves to rescue them.[15] Ahmedabad still provides a friendly home to animals, an interesting commentary on the facile correlations in popular Western thought between their extermination and economic progress.

From about the turn of the century the government was concerned that all communities were not being properly represented on the local bodies. In 1900, the Collector, Mr. M. C. Gibb, pointed out that the thirty-three members of the Ah-

[15] Municipal *Proceedings*, 12 Aug. 1896; G.D. 109/1912; G.D. comp. 360/1914; Municipal *Compilation*, Slaughter-houses (I).

medabad Municipality comprised: one Jew (a proportion of
1 in 102), five Parsis (1 in 143), four Europeans (1 in 158),
eight Jains (1 in 1,587), twelve Hindus (1 in 8,336), and three
Muslims (1 in 10,085).[16] In the previous forty years the proportion of Muslims on the Commission had been steadily
declining, and, still more, their active participation in its dis-
cussions. By the 1880s usually only one or two were attending
the quarterly meetings, and by the 1890s often none at all,
whereas in earlier years three or four had attended. This reflected the continued general decline of the significance of the
Muslim elite in the affairs of Ahmedabad. But in 1915, when
an elective Municipality was restored in Ahmedabad, two seats
were reserved for Muslim candidates and in 1924 this was increased to ten. In 1941 and 1946 there were communal riots
in Ahmedabad, accompanied by killings. This was largely an
echo of the trouble elsewhere and much of it was the doing
of non-Gujaratis, who had come to work in the mill industry.
Ahmedabad was being drawn into the troubles of Indian na-
tionhood and Indian democracy.

In 1960 Ahmedabad once again became a political capital,
this time as the temporary capital of the new State of Gujarat
in independent India. It is again a metropolis, covering an area
of forty square miles on both sides of the Sabarmati, with (at
the 1961 census) a population of 1,156,721. In the provision of
amenities such as gardens, parks, playgrounds, stadiums, audi-
toriums, libraries, museums, and art galleries, Ahmedabad had
previously lagged far behind even such poorly provided cities
as Bombay and Calcutta, but in the last decade especially it
has leaped forward. Its Municipal Corporation has an efficient
programme of educational, health, and recreational services,
and the Ahmedabadis are now applying their talent for efficient organization to goals other than those that were involved

[16] Collector to Commissioner, 17 Aug. 1900 (Municipal *Report*,
1899–1900) (II).

in their highly successful adaptation to modern industry in the
late nineteenth century. The textile industry has established the
Ahmedabad Textile Industry's Research Association and the
city remains the Indian leader in textile quality and design.
Now some diversification of industry is taking place, particularly into chemicals, since the output of the mills has been
limited by the national policy to develop industry elsewhere
in the country. Appropriately, too, the Indian Institute of Management is located in Ahmedabad. But in the last decade, Ahmedabad has been paying more attention to the arts than it
has done for centuries. Its architecture has again achieved distinction by Indian and international standards. Several public
and private buildings were designed by Le Corbusier, including
a cultural centre, and Ahmedabad now has distinguished archi-
tects of its own, notably Doshi. Just as it was in the sixteenth
century, Ahmedabad is again one of the most prosperous and
attractive cities in India.

Glossary

This list of local terms is provided for the convenience of the readers of this book, and does not purport to be applicable in other contexts. Fuller explanations of many of the terms are given in the text. It must be emphasized that usage and spelling vary from time to time and place to place.

ahimsa	non-injury
amir	a high Mughal officer
ant	fictitious mercantile currency
ashram	centre for community living and service
bania	merchant
Bhangi	caste of sweepers and scavengers
chawl	block of tenements

Daskroi	land around city
dharmsala	rest house provided as a charity
diwan	minister, head of revenue administration
faujdar	a police officer
hartal	stoppage of work as a protest
haveli	fort near gate of city
hundi	cheque for payment over distance
karkhana	handicraft factory
khalkuva	cesspool
kazi	Muslim judge
kinkhab	rich cloth embroidered with gold and silver thread
mahajan	guild
maharaj	spiritual head of Vaishnava sect
mansabdar	a Mughal officer
mofussil	the part of the province away from the capital city
mukadam	jobber
nagarseth	city head
octroi	duty on trade of city
panch	artisan guild
panchayat	court of arbitration
panjarapol	animal home
patel	head of artisan guild, headman of village
Patidar	a Hindu caste, originally those among Kanbi agriculturists jointly responsible for payment of land revenue
pol	group of houses
pura	suburb or ward
raj	rule
ryot	subject, peasant
sahukar	financier
sanad	deed of grant
saraf	financier

satyagraha   Gandhian non-violent resistance
seth   head of trade guild, any big financier, mer-
                  chant, or millowner, the leader of a pol
subahdar   governor
swadeshi   Indian-made
taluqdar   holder of an estate
Vania   a Hindu or Jain mercantile caste
Vaishnava   a Hindu sect
zamindar   holder of an estate

Bibliography

I. UNPUBLISHED OFFICIAL RECORDS

Ahmedabad Municipal Corporation, Record Room.

Ahmedabad Municipality. *Proceedings, 1856–1921. Compilations:* Government Resolutions of Education, Financial, General, Judicial, Public Works, Revenue, Revenue (Famine Branch) Departments; Miscellaneous (elections); Miscellaneous (public institutions); Slaughter-houses; Telephone and Tramway; Water Works.

Maharashtra State Record Office, Bombay.

Bombay Government Files. Financial Department, 1882–83; General Department, 1821–1916 (most of the government's municipal proceedings were transacted in the General Department); Judicial Department, 1818–1916 (including *Reports on Native Papers published in the Bombay Presidency and Berar*); Legislative Department, 1894; Political Department, 1816–1820, 1853–1857; Public Department, 1818–1821; Revenue Department, 1818–1916; Revenue Department (Famine Branch), 1896–1903; Secret Department, 1780–1817.

    Baroda Government Affairs, 1816–1819, Selections from the Records of the Bombay Government (not printed), Vol. 145.

National Archives of India, New Delhi.

    Proceedings, Home Department (Education), 1868.

    Proceedings, Home Department (Political), 1919–1920.

    Proceedings, Revenue and Agriculture Department (Surveys), April 1882, B. 11. Completion Report of the Ahmedabad Survey.

India Office Library, London.

    Maps of Ahmedabad, 1809, circa 1822, circa 1850, 1917.

II. OFFICIAL PUBLICATIONS

Ahmedabad Municipality. *Report*. Ahmedabad, annually, 1882–1920.

Bombay Government. *Correspondence Regarding City Surveys in Gujarat under Act IV, 1868. (Selections from the Records of the Bombay Government*, Vol. CXXXV, new series.)

——. *Gazetteer of the Bombay Presidency*, Vol. II: *Surat and Broach, 1877*, Vol. III: *Kaira and Panch Mahals, 1879*, Vol. IV: *Ahmedabad, 1879*, Vol. VI: *Rewa Kantha, Narukot, Cambay, and Surat States, 1880*, Vol. VII: *Baroda, 1883*, Vol. VIII: *Kathiawar, 1884*, Vol. IX, Parts 1 and 2: *Gujarat Population, 1901 and 1899*. Bombay, 1877–1901.

——. *General Report on the Administration of the Bombay Presidency for the years 1872–1873*. Bombay, 1873.

——. *Papers Relating to the Revision Survey Settlement of 123 Villages of the Daskroi Taluka of the Ahmedabad Collectorate. (Selections from the Records of the Bombay Government*, CCXIV, new series.) Bombay, 1889.

——. *Provincial Report on the Working of the Indian Factories Act for the Year.* . . . Bombay, annually 1888–1902.

——. *Report of the Commissioners Appointed by the Governor of Bombay in Council to enquire into the conditions of the Operatives in the Bombay Factories, and the necessity or otherwise for the Passing of a Factory Act.* Bombay, 1875.

——. *Report on Municipal Taxation and Expenditure in the Bombay Presidency for the year....* Bombay, annually, 1878–1898.

——. *Royal Commission on Indian Labour. Memorandum from the Government of Bombay, 1929.* Bombay, 1929.

——. *Source Material for a History of the Freedom Movement in India.* Vols. I, II. Bombay 1957, 1958.

Cruikshank, J. *Report on the Portion of the Duskroee Purgunna Situated in the Ahmedabad Collectorate, 1825. (Selections from the Records of the Bombay Government,* Vol. X, old series.) Bombay, 1853.

Disorders Inquiry Committee. *Report,* Vol. II: *Evidence.* Calcutta, 1920.

Ducat, W. M. *Report on the Water Supply and Sewerage of the City of Ahmedabad.* Ahmedabad, 1885.

Education Commission. *Evidence,* Vol. II. Bombay, 1884.

Fardunji Cooverji. *Report on the Ahmedabad Water-Works.* Ahmedabad, 1892.

Fawcett, E. G. *Report on the Collectorate of Ahmedabad, 1849. (Selections from the Records of the Bombay Government,* Vol. V, new series. Bombay, 1854.)

Government of India. *Imperial Gazetteer of India* (Provincial Series), Vol. I: *Bombay Presidency.* Calcutta, 1909.

Government of India, Census Commissioner. *Census of India* Vol. IX: *1901;* Vol. VII, Part 1: *1911;* Vols. VIII, IX: *1921;* Vol. VIII: *1931.*

Government of Maharashtra. *Mahatma Gandhi. Source Material for a History of the Freedom Movement in India.* Vol. III (Pt. 1). Bombay, 1965.

Indian Factory Commission, 1890. *Report.* Calcutta, 1890.

Indian Factory Labour Commission. *Report. (Parliamentary Papers* 1908, LXXIV, Cd. 4292.)

———. *Evidence*. (*Parliamentary Papers* 1909, LXIII, Cd. 4519.)

Indian Famine Commission, 1901. *Report*, Appendix, Vol. I and II (*Evidence of Witnesses, Bombay Presidency*). Calcutta, 1901.

Indian Industrial Commission, 1916–1918. *Report*, Vol. IV: *Minutes of Evidence*. Calcutta, 1918.

Labour Commission, 1892. *Evidence, Labour Foreign*. (*Parliamentary Papers* 1892, XXXVI, Part V.)

Parliamentary Papers, 1840, VIII, 275.

Report (and Evidence) of the Select Committee appointed to inquire into the Finance and Financial Administration of India, 1871–1874, Vol. III. (*Parliamentary Papers 1873*, XII, 354.)

III. OTHER WORKS

This bibliography includes works which pertain to the history of the city of Ahmedabad, and also general or comparative works cited in the text. The latter are marked with an asterisk.

Acharya, Hemlata. "Creative Response in Indian Economy: A Comment," *Economic Weekly*, IX (27 April, 1957) 547–549.

Ahmedabad Millowners' Association. *Report*, annually (1922–1930).

Ali Muhammad Khan. *Mirat-i-Ahmadi: A Persian History of Gujarat*. Circa 1761. Translated by M. F. Lokhandwala. Baroda, 1965.

* Altekar, A. S. "A History of the Important Ancient Towns and Cities in Gujarat and Kathiawad from Earliest Times to about 1300 A.D.," *Indian Antiquary*, LIII, LIV (1924–25).

Anstey, V. *The Economic Development of India*. 4th ed. London, 1952.

Arnold, E. *India Revisited*. London, 1886.

Badshah, B. D. *The Life of Rao Bahadur Ranchorelal Chhotalal, C. I. E.* Bombay, 1899. In English and Gujarati.

———. *An Elegy on the Death of Shet Madavlal Ranchorelal*. Ahmedabad, 1902. In English and Gujarati.

* Bhargava, B. K. *Indigenous Banking in Ancient and Medieval India.* Bombay, 1935.

Birdwood, G. C. M. *The Industrial Arts of India.* 2 Vols. London, 1880.

Boman-Behram, B. K. (ed.). *The Rise of Municipal Government in the City of Ahmedabad.* Bombay, 1937.

Briggs, H. G. *The Cities of Gujarashtra.* Bombay, 1849.

Buist, G. "Notes on a Journey Through Part of Kattiawar and Goozerat in January 1855," *Transactions of the Bombay Geographical Society,* XIII (1856–57).

Burgess, J. *The Muhammadan Architecture of Gujarat,* Parts I and II (*Archaeological Survey of Western India,* Vols. VII, VIII.) London, 1900, 1905.

Caine, W. S. *Picturesque India.* London, 1890.

Carnac, J. R. "Some Account of the Famine in Guzerat in the years 1812 and 1813," *Transactions of the Literary Society of Bombay,* I (1819).

Carpenter, J. E. *The Life and Work of Mary Carpenter.* London, 1879.

Carpenter, M. *Six Months in India.* 2 Vols. London, 1868.

Commissariat, M. S. *Studies in the History of Gujarat.* Bombay, 1935.

———. "Imperial Mughal Farmans in Gujarat," *Journal of the University of Bombay,* IX, 1 (1940).

———. *A History of Gujarat.* 2 Vols. (1297–1573 and 1573–1758.) Bombay, 1938 and 1957.

———. *Mandelslo's Travels in Western India.* London, 1931.

Crawley-Boevey, A. W. *A Scheme for the Protection and Conservation of Ancient Buildings in and about the City of Ahmedabad.* Bombay, 1886.

Curtis, W. E. *Modern India.* Chicago, 1905.

Dalpatram Dahyabhai. *Dalpat Kavya.* (4th ed.) Vol. II. Edited by H. T. Parekh. Ahmedabad, 1924. In Gujarati.

* Dani, A. H. *Dacca: A Record of its Changing Fortunes.* Dacca, 1957.

Darukhanawala, H. D. *Parsi Lustre on Indian Soil*, Vol. II. Bombay, 1963.

Davar, F. C. *Sir Nowroji P. Vakil: A Biographical Sketch*. Ahmedabad, 1955.

del Mar, W. *India of Today*. London, 1905.

Desai, Mahadev H. *A Righteous Struggle (A Chronicle of the Ahmedabad Textile Labourers' Fight for Justice)*. Ahmedabad, 1951.

Desai, Natvarlal N. *Directory of Ahmedabad Mill Industry, 1929 to 1933, 1934 to 1937, 1929 to 1956*. Ahmedabad, 1935, 1938, 1958.

———. *Industrial Investors' Diary*, Vol. I. Ahmedabad, 1940.

Desai, Neera. *Woman in Modern India*. Bombay, 1957.

———. "Gujarati Society in Nineteenth Century, An Analysis of Social Change." Unpublished Ph.D. thesis, M.S. University of Baroda, 1964.

Desai, Pranlal K. and Hiralal T. Parekh. *Ahmedabad Municipality Shatabdi Smarak Granth* (Centenary Commemoration Volume). Ahmedabad, 1935. In Gujarati.

Deshpande, C. D. "Cities and Towns of Bombay Province: Aspects of Urban Geography," *Indian Geographical Journal*, XVI, 3 (1941).

* Dutt, B. B. *Town Planning in Ancient India*. Calcutta, 1925.

* Dutt, R. Palme. *India Today*. Bombay, 1947.

Edalji Dosabhai. *A History of Gujarat: from the Earliest Period to the Present Time*. Ahmedabad, 1894.

Edwardes, S. M. *Memoir of Rao Bahadur Ranchhodlal Chhotalal, C.I.E.* Exeter, 1920.

Enthoven, R. E. *The Tribes and Castes of Bombay*. 3 Vols. Bombay, 1920.

Forbes, J. *Oriental Memoirs*. 4 Vols. London, 1913.

Forbes-Lindsay, C. H. *India Past and Present*, Vol. II. Philadelphia, 1903.

Forrest, G. W. *Cities of India, Past and Present*. London, 1903.

Fukazawa, H. "Cotton Mill Industry," V. B. Singh (ed.), *Economic History of India 1857–1956*. Bombay, 1965.

Gadgil, D. R. *The Industrial Evolution of India*. 4th ed. Bombay, 1942.

——. *Origins of the Modern Indian Business Class: An Interim Report*. New York, 1959.

Gandhi, M. K. *An Autobiography or The Story of My Experiments with Truth*. 2nd ed. Ahmedabad, 1940.

——. *The Collected Works of Mahatma Gandhi*, Vols. 14, 15 and 16. New Delhi, 1965.

Gandhi, M. P. *The Indian Cotton Textile Industry: Its Past, Present and Future*. Calcutta, 1930.

Gense, J. H. and D. R. Banaji (eds.). *Anandrao Gaikwad, 1814–1819*. (*The Gaikwads of Baroda: English Documents*, Vol. IX.) Bombay, n.d.

Gujarat Vernacular Society. *Annual Report*, 1849, 1854, 1855.

* Habib, I. *The Agrarian System of Mughal India, 1556–1707*. New York, 1963.

* Hagen, E. E. *On the Theory of Social Change: How Economic Growth Begins*. Homewood, Illinois, 1962.

* Heber, R. *Narrative of a Journey Through the Upper Provinces of India from Calcutta to Bombay, 1824–1825*. 2 Vols. London, 1828.

Heimsath, C. H. *Indian Nationalism and Hindu Social Reform*. Princeton, 1964.

Hope, T. C. and J. Fergusson. *Architecture at Ahmedabad, the Capital of Goozerat*. London, 1866.

Hopkins, E. W. "Ancient and Modern Hindu Guilds," *India: Old and New*. New York, 1901.

Houston, J. *Representative Men of the Bombay Presidency*. 2nd ed. Bombay, 1900.

* Hunter, W. W. *Murshidabad and Pabna*. (*A Statistical Account of Bengal*, Vol. IX.) London, 1876.

Indian National Congress. *Report of the Eighteenth Indian National Congress*. Ahmedabad, 1902.

The Indian Textile Journal, 1890–1965. Various articles, especially "Ahmedabad," in Vol. VI, no. 61 (October 1895), and "The Textile Industry in Ahmedabad: A Historical Review," nine articles by 'Shyam-Sundir' (Natverlal G. Parekh) in Vols. XLI and XLII (December 1930–April 1932).

The Indian Textile Journal, Special Souvenir Number. Bombay, 1954.

Irwin, J. "Indian Textile Trade in the Seventeenth Century," *Journal of Indian Textile History*, I (1955).

* Jain, L. C. *Indigenous Banking in India*. London, 1929.

* Kane, P. V. *History of Dharmasastra*, Vol. III. Poona, 1946.

Karnik, V. B. *Indian Trade Unions: A Survey*. 2nd ed. Bombay, 1966.

Krishnarao Bholanath. *The Life of Bholanath Sarabhai*. Ahmedabad, n.d. In English and Gujarati.

* Lamb, H. "The Indian Merchant," M. Singer (ed.), *Traditional India: Structure and Change*. Philadelphia, 1959.

Lely, F. S. P. *Suggestions for the Better Governing of India: with special reference to the Bombay Presidency*. London, 1906.

Linton Bogle, J. M. *Town Planning in India*. London, 1929.

Lobo, M. "Ahmedabad," *Illustrated Weekly of India*. 10 December 1961.

Lokanathan, P. S. *Industrial Organization in India*. London, 1935.

Lothian, A. C. (ed.). *A Handbook for Travellers in India, Pakistan, Burma, and Ceylon*. 17th ed. (Murray's Guide) London, 1955.

MacKay, A. *Western India: Reports Addressed to the Chambers of Commerce of Manchester, Liverpool, Blackburn, and Glasgow*. London, 1853.

Maganlal Vakhatchand. *Amdavadno Itihasa* (History of Ahmedabad). Ahmedabad, 1851. In Gujarati.

Mahomed Kasim Firishtah. *History of the Rise of the Mahomedan Power in India till the year A.D. 1612*, Vol. IV. Translated by J. Briggs. London, 1829.

Majmudar, M. R. "Social Life and Manners in Pre-British Gujarat." Unpublished Master's thesis. University of Bombay, 1929.

———. *Cultural History of Gujarat; from early times to pre-British period*. Bombay, 1965.

Malabari, B. M. *Gujarat and the Gujaratis: Pictures of Men and Manners Taken from Life*. London, 1882.

Mavalankar, G. V. and C. B. Dalal. *Rashtriya Chalvalman Amdavad Municipalityno Falo* (The Contribution of Ahmedabad Municipality in the National Movement). Ahmedabad, 1962. In Gujarati.

Mehta, K. (ed.). *Ahmedabad, 1958*. Ahmedabad, 1959.

Mehta, S. D. *The Cotton Mills of India, 1854–1954*. Bombay, 1954.

Mehta, Yashodhar. *Ranchhodlal ane bija natako* (Ranchhodlal and other Plays). Ahmedabad, 1948. In Gujarati.

———. "Ahmedabad," *All India Radio Miscellany*, 1959.

———. "Indian Textiles," *Akashvani*, 2 April, 1961.

———. "Indian Cotton Textile Industry. The Pioneers." Talk on All India Radio, Ahmedabad, 21 April 1961 (typescript).

———. "About Ourselves with Apologies. We Gujaratis." Talk on All India Radio, Calcutta, 25 May, 1961 (typescript).

Minayeff, L. P. *Travels in and Diaries of India and Burma*. Calcutta, n.d.

Mohanlal Dalpatram Dahyabhai. *Purushprayatna ane Ishwarkrupa* (Man's Labour and God's Blessing). Ahmedabad, 1903. In Gujarati.

* Nair, Kusum. *Blossoms in the Dust*. London, 1961.

Nanddas Haridas. "The Cotton Mill Industry of Ahmedabad," *Modern Bombay*. Bombay, 1941.

Narsinhrao Bholanath. *Smaranmukur* (Reminiscences). Bombay, 1926. In Gujarati.

* O'Malley, L. S. S. *Bengal District Gazetteers: Murshidabad*. Calcutta, 1914.

Ookhtomsky, E. *Travels in the East of Nicholas II, Emperor of Russia, when Cesarewitch 1890–1891*. London, 1891.

Pandit, D. P. "Creative Response in Indian Economy: A Regional Analysis," *Economic Weekly*, IX (23 Feb. and 2 March, 1957.) pp. 283–86, 315–17.

Pandya, B. V. *Striving for Economic Equality*. Bombay, 1959.

Panjabi, K. L. *The Indomitable Sardar*. 2nd ed. Bombay, 1964.

Parekh, Bansidhar Govardhandas. *Seth Mangaldas Girdhardas*

Jivan ane Karya (Seth Mangaldas Girdhardas: His Life and Work). Ahmedabad, 1955. In Gujarati.

Parekh, Hiralal T. *Gujarat Vernacular Society no Itihasa* (History of the Gujarat Vernacular Society). 3 Vols. Ahmedabad, 1932, 1933, 1934. In Gujarati.

Parikh, Narhari D. *Sardar Vallabhbhai Patel*, Vol. I. Ahmedabad, 1953.

Parikh, Ramlal (ed.). *Souvenir: 66th Session Indian National Congress*. Bhavnagar, 1961.

Pavlov, V. I. *The Indian Capitalist Class: a historical study*. New Delhi, 1964.

Pearse, A. S. *The Cotton Industry of India, being the Report of the Journey to India*. Manchester, 1930.

Playne, S. *The Bombay Presidency, the United Provinces, the Punjab etc. Their History, People, Commerce, and Natural Resources*. London, 1917–1920.

*Pocock, D. F. "The Movement of Castes," *Man*, LV (May, 1955) 71–72.

*——. "Sociologies: Urban and Rural," *Contributions to Indian Sociology*, No. 4 (April, 1960).

Ratnamanirao Bhimrao Jhote. *Gujaratnu Patnagar—Amdavad* (Ahmedabad, the Capital of Gujarat). Ahmedabad, 1929. In Gujarati.

——. *Amdavadno Parichay* (Introducing Ahmedabad). Ahmedabad, 1936. In Gujarati.

——. *Ahmedabad and Other Places of Interest in Gujarat*. Ahmedabad, n.d.

*Redfield, R. and M. Singer. "The Cultural Role of Cities," *Economic Development and Cultural Change* Vol. III, No. 1 (1954).

Rice, A. K. *Productivity and Social Organization: The Ahmedabad Experiment*. London, 1958.

Rogers, A. *The Land Revenue of Bombay: A History of its Administration, Rise, and Progress*. 2 Vols. London, 1892.

Rotary Club of Ahmedabad. *Ahmedabad*. Ahmedabad, 1940.

Rousselet, L. *India and its Native Princes*. London, 1882.

Samuelson, J. *India Past and Present*. London, 1890.

Saran, P. *The Provincial Government of the Mughals (1526–1658)*. Allahabad, 1941.

Sastry, N. S. R. *A Statistical Study of India's Industrial Development*. Bombay, 1947.

Sen, Surendranath (ed.). *Indian Travels of Thevenot and Careri*. New Delhi, 1949.

* Shah, A. M. "Political System in Eighteenth Century Gujarat," *Enquiry*, Vol. I, No. 1 (Spring, 1964) pp. 83–95.

Shankerlal Amritray. *Amdavadno Jivan Vikas* (Expansion of Ahmedabad City). Ahmedabad, 1921. In Gujarati.

Sharma, T. R. *Location of Industries in India*. 3rd ed. Bombay, 1954.

Shukla, H. S. *Ahmedabad Guide*. Ahmedabad, 1941.

* Sinha, N. C. *Studies in Indo-British Economy Hundred Years Ago*. Calcutta, 1940.

* Sinha, N. K. *The Economic History of Bengal from Plassey to the Permanent Settlement*, Vol. II. Calcutta, 1962.

Spate, O. H. K. *India and Pakistan: A General and Regional Geography*. 2nd ed. London, 1957.

Spodek, H. "The 'Manchesterisation' of Ahmedabad." *Economic Weekly*, XVII (13 March, 1965) pp. 483–90.

Syed Nawab Ali and S. N. Seddon. *The Supplement to the Mirat-i-Ahmedi*. Baroda, 1924.

* Taylor, J. *A Sketch of the Topography and Statistics of Dacca*. Calcutta, 1840.

Thoothi, N. A. *The Vaishnavas of Gujarat*. Calcutta, 1935.

* Tinker, H. *The Foundations of Local Self-Government in India, Pakistan and Burma*. London, 1954.

Tiwari, R. D. *Railway Rates in Relation to Trade and Industry in India*. Bombay, 1937.

Toy, S. *The Strongholds of India*. London, 1957.

Trivedi, A. B. *Post-War Gujarat: an Economic Survey after World War II*. Bombay, 1949.

Trivedi, U. K. "Social Reform in Gujarat: a Retrospect," *Indian Review*, Vol. VI, No. 12 (December 1905).

Tyrwhitt, J. (ed.). *Patrick Geddes in India.* London, 1947.

Vallabhji Sundarji Punjabhai *Rajnagarnan Ratno* (Jewels of the Capital): *Representative Men of the Ahmedabad City.* Rajkot, 1918. In Gujarati.

Vaupell, J. "Desultory Notes and Observations on Various Places in Guzerat and Western India," *Transactions of the Bombay Geographical Society*, VII (1844–1846).

* Walsh, J. H. T. *A History of Murshidabad District (Bengal) with biographies of some of its noted families.* London, 1902.

Watt, G. *Indian Art at Delhi, 1903.* Calcutta, 1903.

Workman, W. H. and F. B. *Through Town and Jungle.* London, 1904.

Yajnik, Indulal K. *Gandhi as I Know Him.* New Edition. Delhi, 1943.

Yajnik, J. U. *Note on Local Self-Government in the Bombay Presidency.* Bombay, 1882.

Index